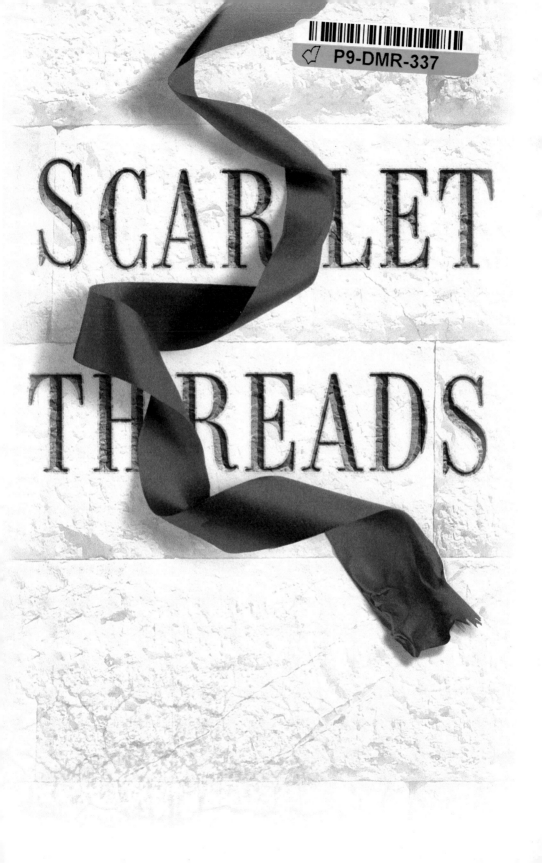

SCARLET THREADS

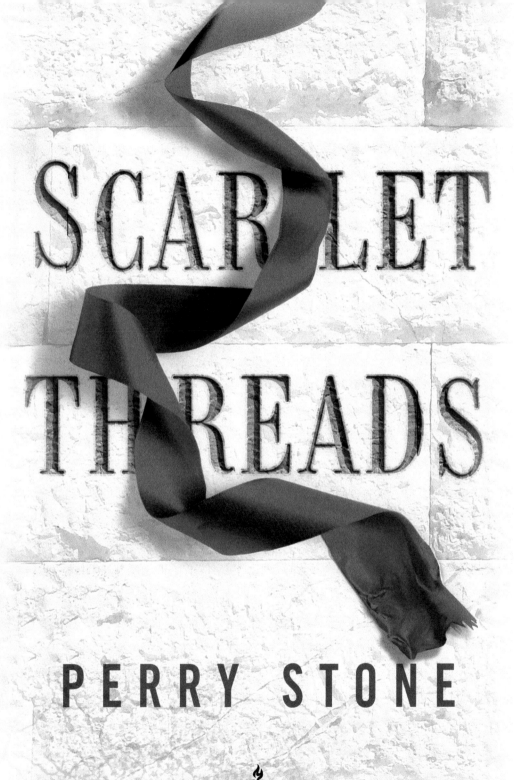

SCARLET THREADS

PERRY STONE

CHARISMA
HOUSE

Visit the author's website at www.voe.org.

Library of Congress Cataloging-in-Publication Data:
Stone, Perry F.
  Scarlet threads / by Perry Stone. -- First edition.
     pages cm
  Includes bibliographical references.
  ISBN 978-1-62136-998-1 (trade paper) -- ISBN 978-1-62136-999-8
(e-book)
  1. Rahab (Biblical figure) 2. Women in the Bible. 3. Mothers--
Religious life. 4. Spiritual life--Christianity. I. Title.
  BS580.R3S76 2014
  220.9'2082--dc23

                                     2014023783

First edition

14 15 16 17 18 — 9 8 7 6 5 4 3 2 1
Printed in the United States of America

CONTENTS

ACKNOWLEDGMENTS

WITH MANY OF my books I reflect a moment and present special acknowledgment to someone whose life example served as an inspiration, assisting me in understanding the subject of the material in the book. In this case, when I read Scarlet Threads, my mind and heart go out immediately to one person—my wife, Pam.

When I wrote about the amazing parallels of Ruth in this book, I thought about my precious Pam. We first met in a four-week revival in 1980 when I was twenty and she was eighteen. After being in her presence for four weeks, I knew I could not live without this woman in my life, thus I married her and have been her husband for more than thirty-three years.

She is the best mom, wife, and friend imaginable, and she has made my life and ministry a joy. I dedicate this book to her and to all the other young Pams out there that God will raise up as great women of God in the future.

CHAPTER 1

A PRAYING MOTHER
WAS A COMMON THREAD

IN THE SIXTY-SIX BOOKS IN THE BIBLE THERE ARE EXAMPLES of men who prayed, and their answers were delayed or denied. Moses's prayer for Miriam was answered seven days after Moses interceded for her healing, yet David's six-day fast and prayer vigil for his infant son to live was denied (Num. 12:10–15; 2 Sam. 12:15–19). However, in these same sixty-six books there is not one example of a *woman* who prayed and did not get God's attention or her prayers answered.

There is *one common thread* that keeps connecting conversion testimonies, especially of men who came to Christ after hanging by a *thread* between life and death, mortality and eternity. Some recalled being so intoxicated that they couldn't remember driving home. Others vividly remembered over-dosing on pills or experiencing a hit of cocaine, sending their heart into overdrive and shooting arrows of fear into their minds as the cold angel of death breathed down their necks.

1

Others relate a living nightmare of the sound of metal on metal clashing in the air, followed by an ambulance crew rushing their broken bodies to an emergency room as they blacked in and out of consciousness, bordering between a chasm of physical life and spiritual death. When these now grown men whom I have met over the years returned from the land of the living dead, and were asked what the main *key* was that moved the hand of God and snatched them from the dark valley of death, lifting them into the light of eternal life, the common thread was always, "It was my Mama's prayers."

In the Bible God cannot resist the prayer of a godly woman, and a godly woman cannot resist communicating with God. Based upon more than three decades of full-time ministry, I have pondered why it seems a woman can *touch* the heart of God, *move* the hand of God, *change* the mind of God, and *attract* the favor of God, it seems, faster than most men. In part I believe it is because men often pray once and move on accepting whatever happens as God's will, while a woman will pray unceasingly until the breakthrough manifests. One consideration worthy of discussion is this: *Christ had an earthly mother but not an earthly father.* His emotional connection was with His mother and His spiritual connection was with His heavenly Father.

According to Scripture, three bear record in heaven: the Father, the Word, and the Spirit (1 John 5:7). God Almighty was and is the Father of the Lord Jesus Christ (Eph. 1:3). However, neither the almighty Father God, nor Christ His Son, nor the Holy Spirit have a heavenly mother, as none of the godhead in their eternal past were birthed through the womb of a female. The entire Trinity—the Father, Son, and Holy Spirit, is all addressed with the pronouns "He," "Him," or "Himself," and never a "she," a "her," or an "it." They are all identified with masculine pronouns. God said, "Let Us make man in Our image, according to Our likeness" (Gen. 1:26). Adam was made in God's image, but Eve was created by God, being taken out of man and formed from Adam's rib. *God never had a mother, and neither did His first man, Adam.* Yet, Christ, who was God in the flesh, called the last Adam (1 Cor. 15:45), *did have an earthly mother.*

God implanted in the womb of the blessed Virgin Mary a seed—not a human seed or sperm, but the seed of God's Word. Thus the Word, "became flesh and dwelt among us" (John 1:14). For nine months God prepared a body for Christ to dwell in, as it is written, "Therefore, when He came into the world, He said: 'Sacrifice and offering You did not desire, but a body You have prepared for Me'" (Heb. 10:5). The ancient prophecy of Isaiah foretold that the Messiah would be born of a virgin (Isa. 7:14), which was required to prevent the sinful corruptible Adamic blood from flowing through the DNA and chromosomes of an earthly father. Christ's blood type was from His heavenly father, just as Adam, a fully grown man, received his blood when God breathed into him the breath of life (Gen. 2:7).

Mary was the *earthly vessel* chosen to carry the *physical body* of the living Son of God. Mary raised Christ in Nazareth, becoming concerned about Him at age twelve when He was missing from the caravan departing from Jerusalem and was found debating in the temple (Luke 2:42–52). Mary heard and saw things that she kept hid in her heart (v. 51). Eighteen years later when Christ began His public ministry, it was His mother who inspired Him to perform His first miracle—turning water into wine, when she instructed the servants, "Whatever He [Jesus] says to you, do it" (John 2:5). It was His mother who faithfully followed His ministry, along with other women named Mary, and like any caring mother who loves her son she was with Him at the foot of the cross during His final moments on earth.

During the six hours of Christ's intense and unbearable suffering, He looked down and saw Mary standing beside His beloved disciple, John. Here was the scene at the cross:

> Now there stood by the cross of Jesus His mother, and His mother's sister, Mary the wife of Clopas, and Mary Magdalene. When Jesus therefore saw His mother, and the disciple whom He loved standing by, He said to His mother, "Woman, behold your son!" Then He said to the disciple, "Behold your mother!" And from that hour that disciple took her to his own home.
> —JOHN 19:25–27

Perhaps at this moment, with the agony Mary felt she recalled a personal prophecy she received from an old rabbi at the temple shortly after Christ's birth. More than thirty-three years prior in Jerusalem, a few hundred yards from where she was now standing, Rabbi Simeon saw the infant Christ and told Mary:

> (Yes, a sword will pierce through your own soul also), that the thoughts of many hearts may be revealed.
> —LUKE 2:35

Christ saw His mother, a woman of flesh and blood who had given Him life, raised Him, followed His ministry, now watching the drama of the ages unfold as scene one of the redemption story was being written in His blood. Christ saw the broken heart of His mother as John led her away just before Christ breathed His last. Christ loves mothers and is drawn to their tears, words, and prayers. After all, He lived in the house, ate her cooking, saw her clean His clothes and His room, and knew she was blessed above all women.

Through a woman, Eve, the Fall came to mankind, but through a woman, Mary, redemption came to the world. Throughout the ancient and modern history of Israel, when the nation hit its most dangerous crises, even to the point of extermination, *God used a woman to deliver the people.* As far back as the prophetess Deborah, who organized an army against invaders, or Esther, the Persian queen whose wisdom and uncanny decision to approach the king spared the Jews from destruction in one hundred twenty-seven provinces, the voices and actions of anointed women who are not afraid to approach the king for intervention never go unnoticed or unheard.

In a modern example, during the darkest moments of the Yom Kippur War, when Israel was caught in a surprise attack by Syrian and Egyptians armies armed with tanks, Israel's female prime minister, Golda Meir, called the United States requesting immediate military assistance, but the secretary of state, Henry Kissinger, had made the statement, "Let the Jews bleed a little." In desperation Golda called President Nixon at the White House at three o'clock in the morning. Her voice reminded Nixon of his Quaker mother, and immediately he responded by providing necessary aircraft and military equipment to turn the war in Israel's favor. Golda refused to give up, and her persistence to make a call at three in the morning Eastern Standard Time may have been the most important phone call in Israel's modern history.[1]

So how are a praying man and a praying woman different? It is the nature of a determined woman to resist settling on *no* as the final answer. This *I won't give up* tenacity is emphasized in a parable in Luke 18, where a judge refused to hear a woman's plea and sent her away without any justice. She continued to pursue the attention of this head civil authority until the judge knew the woman would never quit until he took on her case, and he gave her justice against her adversary (vv. 1–8).

Godly women are the immune system in the church and the nation. They hold the family together. While some parents have moved from face-to-face training up of a child, to a more *electronic parenting system* that includes television, computers, iPads, and video games, God's gift to a child and a husband is a spiritual mother and wife. Praying mothers are the roadblocks that will help keep their family members out of hell.

Praying mothers weave a thread of faith in the heart of their bloodlines, and, as we will see in the next chapter, this scarlet thread was the secret that saved an entire family from destruction and death, setting a path of destiny that would lead a woman, wife, and mother to a famous name and a famous bloodline.

CHAPTER 2

The JEWEL FROM JERICHO

I N JOSHUA'S TIME JERICHO WAS THE JEWEL OF THE Canaanite cities, considered today by archaeologists to be the oldest city on earth, dating back to 10,000 BC. The ancient city was built around a spring of fresh water, a needed source for early nomads and travelers who required the life-giving substance for their animals and themselves. Also called the City of Palms, its geographical location 4.35 miles from the Jordan River, 6.2 miles from the northern part of the Dead Sea, and 18.6 miles from Jerusalem makes it a common stop for travelers over the many millenniums. It is important to note that Jericho is about 32 miles from the city of Bethlehem, which is significant in the Rahab narrative. The city is below sea level and is considered the lowest city on earth.[1] Jericho's first mention in Scripture is when Joshua led the Israelites across the Jordan River (Num. 22:1). The real jewel living within its walls was a woman whose name would one day be listed in the genealogy of the Messiah.

I have viewed the ruins and levels of occupation at the Tel

(hill) of Jericho, where the early buildings were made of clay-backed mud bricks. Later the city was highly fortified with large stones and walls built in the form of terraces, and in ascending levels. The hill where the city was built was surrounded by an earthen embankment. The outer wall was formed of large stones standing between twelve and fifteen feet high. The mud-brick wall was on top, about six feet thick and twenty to twenty-six feet high. The entire living space inside the walls was about nine acres, and the population would have been several thousand.[2]

The city in Joshua's time was a Canaanite city, thus the sins of the Canaanites were prominent within Jericho. The Torah reveals that the inhabitants worshipped idols, and archaeological evidence shows cultic altars were built for the numerous gods and goddesses (Exod. 23:23–24). One common abomination was offering children to the idol Molech, called, "passing your children through the fire" (Ezek. 16:21), resulting in polluting the land with blood (Ps. 106:34–39). When excavating the ruins of ancient Canaanite cities, cultic incense altars and small house idols are common finds when sifting through layers of occupation. The conquest of Jericho was the first judgment of God against the idolatrous Canaanite cities, against their false gods, and the shedding of the blood of innocent infants.

Joshua sent two spies secretly at night to gain information from within the city (Josh. 2:1). To prevent arousing suspicion, they went into the home of the town harlot—a common place for male visitors to lodge. It was there that some interesting information was relayed to these two young Hebrew men.

First she acknowledged that the city inhabitants were terrified and fainthearted because of the reputation of the Hebrew God to defeat His enemies. Second, she and the entire city had heard the miraculous stories of how God opened the Red Sea, and Israel slew the two giant kings, Sihon and Og. If Israel could defeat these two feared kings of the Amorites, Jericho had no chance of survival. Third, Rahab wanted a promise that her father, mother, brothers, and sisters would not be slain in the seizure of the city when the attack began. She asked for a visible token to confirm she would be spared (Josh. 2:1–13).

The Three Instructions

Rahab was given three distinct instructions that conceal practical applications for believers today. Her first instruction was to *keep silent* about the spies' visit (v. 14). Based on a city rumor, the king was already seeking out information about these men, and Rahab's assignment was *not to reveal any details* of the visit or conversation. Her second instruction was to *place a scarlet thread* in the window, which would serve as a sign (token) of the Hebrew soldiers protecting her and her family from being slain (v. 18). Her third instruction was to have everyone *remain inside the house* from the moment the battle began until she was led out by the two men who gave her this promise of protection (v. 19). Here is how these three instructions apply to believers today.

Believers often talk too much and allow people close to us to distort our focus. Instead of focusing on the main issue, we spend time worrying about drowning in a mud puddle. It is one thing to battle a bear and nearly get mauled to death with its claws, and an entirely different things to get stuck in a swamp and have a thousand mosquitoes attempt to bite you to death. If we are not careful, we spend more time discussing the wormy six apples on the tree instead of the hundred healthy ones waiting to be picked. Rahab was given the plan, but she had to refrain from talking about the strategy to others outside of her family. If your focus is saving your family from Satan's destruction, then move from the worms you see—to the root of the tree. There is a reason Scripture instructs us to "hold fast our confession" of faith (Heb. 4:14), and to pray without being double minded or without wavering (James 1:5–8). Confession is always *verbal* and never just mental agreement. Prayer is verbal petitioning but holding on to your prayer centers on confession, which is *maintaining agreement* with your prayer. It is impossible to hold on to something that's not first possessed in your heart.

The Scarlet Thread

The token, or *sign* of Rahab's covenant of protection was a scarlet thread placed in the window. This was not just a scarlet cord, but it was also a faith object, or a point of contact that, as she viewed it days before the battle, gave her comfort and confidence that the promise from the two spies would be fulfilled. I am certain she imagined what life would be like switching *ites* from a *Canaanite* to an *Israelite*. She was unmarried, and the two spies were "young men" (Josh. 6:23). Did she peer through the window, past the scarlet thread, miles away to the thousands of Israelite tents, wondering if her future husband was already marked by the Hebrew God, someone just for her? She was born and dwelt among the Canaanites, but soon she would live in a land renamed Israel (v. 25). Jewish tradition believes she married one of the two spies. God places tools of faith and objects of faith in our lives to encourage us to continue believing the promises.

The scarlet thread was a promise—a covenant reminder. The word *scarlet* is used forty-six times in the Old Testament (KJV). In the Scripture most colors have one specific meaning. Blue is always heavenly; purple is always royalty or kingly; white is always purity. The color scarlet, however, can have a dual meaning. Scarlet can represent both *sin* and *forgiveness*. Isaiah spoke about Israel's sins being as *scarlet*, that are made white as snow (Isa. 1:18). In the Book of Revelation, the woman riding the beast is clothed in scarlet and purple but is identified as the scarlet harlot—a false religion (Rev. 17:4). However, the color scarlet is also associated with the color of blood—thus a picture of the precious blood of Christ. In the curtains of the tabernacle there were three layers on the covering of the holy place, including one of goat's skin dyed scarlet, representing the atoning blood of animals on the brass altar, which would be the means of forgiveness for Israel.

One of the most bizarre narratives in the Bible is about the double deaths of Judah's two sons. The story is inserted between the betrayal of Joseph by his brothers (Gen. 37), and Joseph being purchased in Egypt (Gen. 39). In the story found in Genesis 38 Judah married off one of his sons, Er, to a woman named Tamar. However, Er was stricken for his wickedness and suddenly died. Judah's second son, Onan, married Tamar, but was unwilling to carry on his brother's name by having a son through her, and so he was also slain by God. Judah had a third younger son, Shelah, whom he promised to Tamar, but some suggest Judah was afraid to give him to Tamar in marriage, fearful he too would die. After all, when two boys from the same family marry the same woman and end up dead, that's not good advertisement for a new husband.

After denying her the third son, Tamar posed as a prostitute and went into Judah, becoming pregnant with twins. The birth of a firstborn among twins was marked, as the firstborn son received both the birthright and the blessing of the father. When the time came for their birth, one infant put his hand out and the midwife marked it by tying to his tiny arm a scarlet thread. However, at the time of birth, the other twin, a son to be named Perez, came out first. This was the first reference to a scarlet thread.

In the Old Testament the common Hebrew word for *scarlet* is *towla.* The Hebrew word comes from a root for a type of *worm*, which was crushed and produced a special red dye. This worm called towla, or the *coccus ilicis*, was believed to be used as the dye for the original color in the Jewish tallits. For centuries this worm was unknown, until researchers discovered it again several years ago in Israel.

These worms do not look like our traditional worms but are small, shaped like a bean, and grow on plants, looking like a part of the plant itself. The female worm gives birth once in her lifetime. After laying eggs on some type of wood—a tree or fencepost—she becomes so attached that she can only be physically removed by tearing her body apart. The tiny worms stay under the protective covering of their mother's shell as they feed off the body of the mother. After the baby worms mature, the mother dies while secreting a red substance that can be used as a dye. This red stain will remain on these worms the rest of their lives. After three days the mother's body turns white, and her remains fall to the ground. In ancient times the remains of crimson worms were scraped from trees, dried, and the crushed powder was used to dye cloth or garments the color red.[3]

Interestingly in Psalms 22 there is a series of Messianic prophecies in which the Messiah is called "a worm, and no man; a reproach of men, and despised by the people" (v. 6). The Hebrew word *worm* here is *towla*, the actual Hebrew name for this crimson-colored worm. The natural characteristics of this worm are parallel to Christ's suffering. Christ died on a tree, broken and bleeding, but in three days He arose, and through faith His red blood washes us clean. Isaiah spoke of God's cleansing power this way:

> "Come now, and let us reason together,"
> Says the LORD,
> "Though your sins are like scarlet,

They shall be as white as snow;
Though they are red like crimson,
They shall be as wool."

—Isaiah 1:18

God required blue fringes on the four corners of the Jewish prayer covering called the *tallit*. The tradition states that the original Ten Commandments were carved by God's hand upon sapphire stones, and as devout Jewish men looked upon the blue threads they were reminded of the laws inscribed upon the stone sapphire tablets. According to the Temple Institute in Jerusalem, the blue dye used to color the fringes of the tallit was derived from snails found in the Mediterranean Sea, the huge body of water off the coasts of Israel. The rarity of the snail and the cost of producing the dye caused the Romans to issue decrees that only royalty could wear the blue-dyed garments. Because of political and cost issues, by the second century AD the blue fringes were omitted from the tallits, and the secret of the dye was lost.[4]

Several years ago at a Samaritan Village, Neve Tsuf, individuals from the Temple Institute in Jerusalem, an organization researching temple history, rituals, and sacred furniture, organized an event in which they gathered a harvest of the of the *tola'at shani*, the crimson worms necessary to color the belt of the priestly garments, the scarlet wool for the scapegoat, and the scarlet thread needed when burning a red heifer. After ten years of diligently researching historical detail and the locations of the worms for the biblical dyes, Professor Zohar Amar discovered two locations: one in Turkey, the other in South America. However, he was amazed to discover that what he was looking for was about fifty feet from his front door, nesting in an oak tree. The worm is not a worm in the literal sense but more of a small insect. The red secretion has now been used to dye threads being used to make reproductions of the priestly garments at the institute.[5]

At the Jerusalem temple on the Day of Atonement, three scarlet threads were used in the atonement ritual. Two identical goats were selected; one for the altar of sacrifice and one which would have hands laid upon it as priests led it into the wilderness. A third thread was nailed to the outer door of the temple. Once the goat carrying sins was pushed off a cliff in the Judean Wilderness, the red thread on the temple door turned white and the people rejoiced knowing their sins had been forgiven. Jewish sources indicate that the red thread ritual continued to be used up to the time of the destruction of the temple. However, forty years before the destruction (this would be about AD 70), the red thread never turned white again for forty years.[6]

The scarlet thread of Rahab is a picture of redemption through Christ's blood. On the roof of Rahab's house were piles of flax and dyed threads, some crimson or scarlet colored. This dye required for scarlet would have likely come from the towla worm, from which the crimson color originated. Since the worm itself is a picture of the Messiah, whose red blood would cleanse the sinner and bring redemption, the hanging of the red thread in a window that could be seen by the invading Israelites was a perfect preview of Christ, whose blood and suffering was a public spectacle, yet those who look to the Christ of the cross have a promise of deliverance from death. (See John 5:24.)

The House on the Wall

The third fact that ensured the safety of Rahab's entire family rested in their obedience to remain inside the house, which had been marked by the scarlet thread. This reminds us of forty-one years prior at the time of the Exodus when the outer posts of the *doors* were marked by the lamb's blood, preventing the destroying angel from entering the home and slaying the firstborn (Exod. 12). In Rahab's case, a single window where the spies were lowered was marked by a scarlet cord, which was large enough for the Hebrew warriors to see.

The biblical narrative reveals the location of Rahab's house, "...for her house was on the city wall; she dwelt on the wall" (Josh. 2:15). From the windows of her house she could see the caravans, including any men entering the city gates. Prior to the conquest of Jericho, she no doubt looked from inside to the outside, observing the Jordan River dividing the land and the hundreds of thousands of Hebrew families setting up camp in Gilgal. They looked like miles of swarming locusts covering the ground. The scarlet thread was attached inside the window. On the seventh day the Israelites shouted with a great shout and entered the fortified city, and the wall of the city fell down flat, "and the army will go up, everyone straight in" (Josh. 6:5, NIV). The walls of Jericho were built in several layers and tiers, with Rahab's house possibly on the top tier. *When the wall collapsed, her home remained intact.*

Staying in the house was required while the battle raged. For six days Israel circled Jericho, saying nothing. On the seventh day the ram's horns blew, the people shouted, and the walls trembled, falling down flat. Suddenly Rahab's family could hear the mixed sounds of screaming and the clash of metal swords, but the power of death was restrained, just as it was forty-one years earlier when the Hebrews had placed the lamb's blood on the left, right, and top outer posts of the door, stopping the angel of death cold in its tracks.

Just as Rahab's house was preserved in the battle, Christ predicted that the gates (strategies) of hell would not prevail against the church. The church is not so much a building or a denomination as it is a unit of believers who assemble as a family to study the

Bible and worship God. There are areas in America where there are no full gospel churches for hundreds of miles as only small communities exist. The churches are often small home Bible studies. In Communist nations the true Christian church often meets underground, in caves, back rooms of factories, or in thick forests and rugged mountains. In these nations the churches are growing and are a living organism as Communism, fanatical Islam, and false religions cannot prevail against the body of Christ.

The Wall, the Rope, and the Basket

The New Testament tells a story about Paul that carries a similar message to the story of Rahab's scarlet thread, for it also gives a picture of redemption. Luke wrote about Paul's narrow escape with death in Damascus, Syria, shortly after his conversion:

> Now after many days were past, the Jews plotted to kill him. But their plot became known to Saul. And they watched the gates day and night, to kill him. Then the disciples took him by night and let him down through the wall in a large basket.
> —ACTS 9:23–25

Here is a question. What was the single most important element in this story: the strength and height of the wall, the size and the circumference of the basket, or the length of the rope? Obviously the basket was perfect as it held Paul's entire body, and the height of the wall was insignificant as the rope was strong enough to hold Paul's weight and long enough to reach the bottom. The most important part of this story was...*the men who were holding the rope.* When Paul stepped into the basket, his physical life was placed in the hands of those gripping the rope, feeling the body weight of Paul as the basket slowly slid down the city wall. With one slip of the rope, the basket would break apart against the wall, crashing to the bottom, injuring the apostle.

As I grew up in a full gospel denomination, I observed two major prayers that were prayed every week, especially on Sunday morning among the believers who gathered. With the majority of congregations having members over fifty-five years of age, there were always requests for *physical healing*, including members and friends in the hospital or recovering at home, unable to attend church. The second most common prayer was to "remember" a husband or a child (or children) that was "lost" (unconverted) and who needed Christ. The majority of requests for children came from mothers, as a godly mother finds it impossible to remove herself from off the wall when her child is dangling in a basket between life and death. The rope holders are grace givers under pressure. They refuse to slip in their Bible reading, in their intercession, and in their love for the child in the basket. Jewish history teaches that Miriam, the sister of Moses, watched over the river where the tiny ark holding her infant brother was floating on the waters. Miriam "held on to the rope," becoming a guardian of mercy, until her baby brother was in the hands of Pharaoh's daughter.

The Battle for Eternal Life

Everything that emits from God contains life. In the Old Testament the Hebrew word for *life* is *chay*, referring to the God life in animals and plants. The tree that sustained Adam and Eve in the garden was called the Tree of Life. In the Greek there are three words translated as life: *bios*, *psuche*, and *zoa*. The word *bios* is the root word for biology, and refers to all living forms. The word *psuche* deals with the mind and emotions, and *zoe* is the highest form of life, used in the New Testament to refer to the life of God and eternal life. In John 12:25 a rather unusual verse can be better interpreted when understanding the Greek words used for "life."

> He who loves his life will lose it, and he who hates his life in
> this world will keep it for eternal life.

The man who loves his *life* is the Greek word *psuche*, which refers to the mortal life of a person—the temporary life force within the human body that keep a mortal living. If a man loves only his earthly life and ignores his eternal destiny, he abides in death. However, if he refuses to be ruled by his mortal desires he will inherit eternal life—or *zoe*.

There is a mortal and eternal component in every human being. The body is mortal and corruptible, but the spirit is eternal and incorruptible. The will of God is for us to have life more abundantly (John 10:10). There is a difference between eternal life in heaven and abundant life on earth. Eternal life is a gift from God, but abundant life is a choice. Eternal life is God's gift to you, but abundant life is your gift back to God. Eternal life is coming in the future, but abundant life is here and now. Eternal life abides in you, while abundant life is all around you.

God did not create you to live a life of just existing from day to day. He created mental thoughts and even chemicals in the brain to help motivate you toward a more abundant life. The enemy of action is idleness, whose seeds breed boredom, and a life of boredom hinders the release of the feel-good chemicals in the brain. One such chemical is dopamine, which is released in the brain and is in charge of the reward and motivation system in the body. Many individuals, especially youth, stay up late at night sitting in dark rooms, not realizing that without natural sunlight and vitamin D, the natural feel-good chemicals in the body are killed, eventually causing depression and frustration.

This is one explanation as to why chemical and alcohol abuse is common. People become unhappy with their lives and cover their despondency with a counterfeit good feeling that leaves a bigger void than what they had. Part of our motivation in life is having a future that we can look forward to.

Your future is summed up in your dreams and visions: dreams of what can be and visions of what will be. Your vision is what you see before you actually see it. Your passion is what you feel that motivates you to pursue the vision or dream. When a person has no vision or passion, he or she will have a boring existence. With a vision but no passion a person will eventually lose energy to pursue their dream. When there is passion but no vision, a person will become frustrated with a lack of visible evidence.

Holding on to a rope is throwing a scarlet thread to someone who needs to be rescued from spiritual danger. When you have a child who has overdosed on drugs and has been rushed to the emergency room, or you receive a call that your companion has been in a terrible accident, and you are in an emergency waiting room, you must throw out a lifeline and grab on to the *scarlet thread of God's promises* that say, "I shall not die, but live, and declare the works of the LORD" (Ps. 118:17). John wrote, "If anyone sees his brother sinning a sin which does not lead to death, he will ask, and He will give him life for those who commit sin not leading to death" (1 John 5:16). There are specific promises for believers in the Bible that can be woven into a life-saving scarlet cord, tying the truth to the heart of the person or circumstance and pulling that person to safety.

The Female Hall of Faith

Hebrews chapter 11 is called the Hall of Faith, a wonderful chapter that lists Old Testament leaders who operated in great faith. In this list there are fifteen men, beginning with Abel and ending with Samuel (Heb. 11:4, 32). There are only two women mentioned in this roll call of faith heroes—Sarah (v. 11) and Rahab (v. 31). The New Testament mentions Rahab in three different places by three different writers: Matthew, James, and Paul, each giving a specific fact:

> Salmon begot Boaz by Rahab, Boaz begot Obed by Ruth, Obed begot Jesse.
>
> —MATTHEW 1:5

> Likewise, was not Rahab the harlot also justified by works when she received the messengers and sent them out another way?
>
> —JAMES 2:25

> By faith the walls of Jericho fell down after they were encircled for seven days. By faith the harlot Rahab did not perish with those who did not believe, when she had received the spies with peace.
>
> —HEBREWS 11:30–31

In the Old Testament era men and women were justified (made right in God's sight) through their "works of faith." Rahab could have sent the Hebrew spies away, considering the risk she would incur hiding them on her roof for the night. However, she discussed her new faith with them, covered for them, and sent them out a different direction for their protection. These men were covered under flax. They remained under her *covering* until the time to return to the Israelite camp (Josh. 2). Jericho was like a jewel in the valley, as the entrance to Jericho was the gateway to the Promised Land. The real jewel however was an unpolished, rough former prostitute who became a mother in Israel! Rahab was a woman who saved her entire family by using her faith. Her faith seed was *sown* for the protection of others (two spies), and her *harvest* was the protection of her own family. What she did for others, God did for her.

Who have you placed under your covering? Your house is more than a structure of wood and brick. Devout Jews place a small object on the right side of their outer door called a *mezuzah*, concealing specific Scripture verses, marking the entrance and exit of their home, the door, with God's Word. If your house has been consecrated to God, through prayer there is a certain level of protection any person receives as a covering when he or she remains in your dwelling.

When praying for someone in my bloodline, I ask the Lord to keep my children, wife, and family members hedged in under a special family *hedge* and in the watchful eye of any *guardian angel* that is assigned to my family lineage. I base the *hedge principle* upon the spiritual principle in the Book of Job. God assigned a protective hedge to Job (Job. 1:10). This hedge surrounded him and all that he owned, including his seven sons and three daughters. Job's children had nothing to do with this hedge. It was assigned personally to Job as he continually offered burnt offerings as a token of his faith in God's favor (v. 5). His faith placed his bloodline under his covering. As for the angel of protection, when Jacob was blessing his grandsons, Ephraim and Manasseh, he asked God to assign the blessing angel that redeemed him to be with these two sons of Joseph (Gen. 48:13–16). The verse you should claim as your own scarlet thread promise is Psalm 34:7: "The angel of the LORD encamps all around those who fear Him, and delivers them."

Your hedge can be a person God uses to secure your blessing, and your angel can be a human messenger God sends to protect you from danger. Job's hedge was possibly an encampment of angels that prevented Satan from entering Job's life and property. Jacob's angel was a heavenly being that he had wrestled with, giving him a blessing and a name change (Gen. 32:24–30). However, your scarlet thread of faith becomes a token to bring your entire family under your covering as the battles rage all around you. Jewels are those precious souls who are being pulled from the destruction of Jericho. These spiritual principles still apply. Discover your strategy and hide the plans in your heart to prevent your adversary from knowing your thoughts. Enforce the power of the blood of Christ as a hedge of protection as the attacks ensue. Finally, find a church, a body of believers who serve as a place of refuge, and "stay in the house," or remain under a spiritual covering.

Rahab's scarlet thread identified her with the same redemptive and protective Hebrew covenant that was established between Abraham the Hebrew (Gen. 17:4–9) and God and passed on to each generation of Hebrew, father to son (Gen. 17:4–9). Her actions demonstrated her faith, and her faith saved her and her household. This woman was a diamond in the rough who became the shining jewel of Jericho.

CHAPTER 3

JAEL and JUDITH– NAILING TROUBLE in the HEAD

Y EARS AGO AN AUTHOR WROTE A BEST-SELLING BOOK on the Prayer of Jabez. The popularity of the book was not just the prayer itself, but also the fact that few Christians had ever heard the name Jabez, and they were curious as to who this biblical personality was and what made his prayer significant. This prayer was taught and prayed, and numerous books spun off of this one man's prayer to God for success.[1] The prayer reads:

> And Jabez called on the God of Israel saying, "Oh, that You would bless me indeed, and enlarge my territory, that Your hand would be with me, and that You would keep me from evil, that I may not cause pain!" So God granted him what he requested.
>
> —1 CHRONICLES 4:10

If you have not heard of the man Jabez before now, you may not have heard of the woman named Jael and her amazing feats. Her narrative is part of an interesting account in the Book of Judges. Prior to Israel anointing its first king, Saul, in the days of the prophet Samuel, the people did what they perceived was right in their own eyes. This self-appointed righteousness bred weaknesses, leaving open a door of opportunity for sin, deceiving the people into thinking no one, including God, would pay attention to their actions. Without a shepherd there was no leadership direction, and eventually the nation found itself in the hands of enemies. In their bondage they cried out to God for deliverance. In each instance the Lord would raise up one person to spearhead a freedom campaign, breaking oppressive strongholds over His people. These individuals, called judges, were predominantly men who became provoked with seeing Israel's enemies prevail and would direct an uprising geared toward defeating their foes. Gideon, Samson, and Jephthah are three of the more noted men of faith and power (Heb. 11:32).

There are the women whose stories are related in three biblical scrolls, each read yearly at specific Jewish holidays: The Song of Solomon on Passover; the Book of Ruth on Pentecost, and Esther on Purim. In Old Testament stories the male figure is central to the narrative, the deliverance, or is the hero. In these three books the woman becomes the main figure or, in the case of Esther, the heroine whose wisdom and favor saved the Jews. The Song of Solomon is the story of a lover and his bridegroom, with an unnamed shepherdess being Solomon's beloved. In the same company of Esther is a lesser known heroine named Jael.

Those who were raised in Sunday school or in a local church have heard the name or the story recounted of a woman judge named Deborah. After the death of the judge Ehud, the Lord delivered

Israel into the hands of Jabin the Canaanite king who ruled from a huge city in Hazor. His army commander was Sisera, who commandeered nine hundred chariots of iron and who had oppressed Israel for twenty years. After living through two decades of oppressive rule, the people began crying out to the Lord for deliverance (Judg. 4:1–3).

Deborah, a prophetess in the tribe of Ephraim, was judging Israel at this time while sitting under a palm tree (vv. 4–5). From the context of the story, the men of Israel were too fearful and unorganized for battle. Deborah employed the assistance of Barak from the tribe of Naphtali to organize tens of thousands of Israeli troops for battle, bringing them down to the brook Kishon where God would deliver Sisera into their hands. Barak agreed, only if Deborah would team up with him. She then made an interesting prediction that is overlooked by many Bible readers and students. Deborah predicted that Barak would get no glory from this conflict. Deborah said:

> "I will surely go with you; nevertheless there will be no glory for you in the journey you are taking, for the LORD will sell Sisera into the hand of a woman." Then Deborah arose and went with Barak to Kedesh.
>
> —JUDGES 4:9

Deborah was one of six prophetesses alluded to in the Bible. They were Miriam, Deborah, Huldah, Noadiah, Isaiah's wife, and Anna. Other women were not classified as prophetesses, but they performed great feats ensuring Israel's deliverance. The name Jael in Hebrew is *Ya'el*, and is the name for a wild mountain goat. Jael lived in a tent, which indicates she lived more as a nomad. Her name indicates that her family was a more outdoor type family. The Israeli mountain goat, called the *ibex*, survives in rugged and

25

dry terrain, and is very swift and sure footed as it runs from mountain to mountain, making it difficult to catch.

Among Israel's judges and deliverers, God used tools of faith in their hands to assist in the act of defeating the enemies. Throughout the Old Testament there are objects that play into the stories of the patriarchs. With Abraham it is altars and wells. Stones play an important role with Jacob, and goats are linked with deception and betrayal. Clothes (his coat) is a major motif in the life of Joseph. In the Book of Judges for Samson it was the jawbone of a dead donkey swinging wildly in his hand (Judg. 15:16), and for Shamgar his weapon was an ox goad (Judg. 3:31). David's weapon of choice was five smooth stones from a brook (1 Sam. 17:40), and for his mighty man Eleazar it was his sword (2 Sam. 23:10). For Moses, his shepherd's staff became his miracle rod (Exod. 4:17). For Jael, the two tools of deliverance would be a hammer and a nail.

In this battle the brook Kishon flooded and Sisera's nine hundred chariots were caught in the overflow and washed away. Sisera, the commander, escaped, fleeing into the tent of Jael, believing he would be protected by her from the Israeli troops pursuing him. Jael was the wife of Heber the Kenite, and Sisera's decision to end up in this area was based upon a peace agreement with King Jabin and the Kenites (Judg. 4:17). The Kenites were skilled metal smiths, and Sisera may have assumed that by fleeing to the area he would be guaranteed protection and could eventually regroup and recover from this horrific defeat.

As Sisera enters the tent he requests that Jael hide him under a blanket (more than likely a large rug). He asks for water, and she gives him milk. Exhausted from the battle, he falls asleep in her tent. Jael seized this opportunity, using a weapon that a metal smith would use—a hammer and a metal nail that had perhaps been produced by the hands of a Kenite blacksmith. *Thus tools that were in her tent became the weapons of war to defeat her enemy.* For a man to be killed by a woman in the Old Testament era was considered a total embarrassment and humiliation to the man's name and to his descendants that may have already been born.

In the days of Elijah the prophet called fire down from heaven, prayed seven times until rain clouds broke a forty-two-month drought, afterward outrunning the horses of Ahab to Samaria. He received a warning that Jezebel had put a *hit* on him and would soon behead him as she had other prophets. Elijah ran into the wilderness and wanted God to kill him, as he was despondent and depressed, believing he was the lone ranger prophet in Israel. If he had really wanted to die, he could have remained in Samaria, been arrested, and died that same day by beheading, fulfilling Jezebel's death threat. However, this prophet refused to have on his tomb, "He died by the hands of a woman!"

Deborah Sang a Song about Jael

In Judges 5 Deborah sang a poetic song about Israel's victory over the armies of Sisera. This prose dates back to the twelfth century BC. Deborah broke out into singing, crediting, among other things, Jael's assistance in the war victory:

> In the days of Shamgar, son of Anath,
> In the days of Jael,
> The highways were deserted,
> And the travelers walked along the byways.
> Village life ceased, it ceased in Israel,
> Until I, Deborah, arose,
> Arose a mother in Israel....
> Most blessed among women is Jael,
> The wife of Heber the Kenite;
> Blessed is she among women in tents.

He asked for water, she gave milk;
She brought out cream in a lordly bowl.
She stretched her hand to the tent peg,
Her right hand to the workmen's hammer;
She pounded Sisera, she pierced his head,
She split and struck through his temple.
At her feet he sank, he fell, he lay still;
At her feet he sank, he fell;
Where he sank, there he fell dead.

—JUDGES 5:6–7, 24–27

Rabbinical sources give Jael an equal place of respect with the four matriarchs. We read, "She was equal to Sarah, Rebecca, Rachel, and Leah."[2] Another comment reads: "Jethro's good deed was that he received in his house a redeemer who had fled from an enemy (i.e., Moses, who fled from Pharaoh). From his house arose (Jael) who received an enemy (Sisera) who fled from a redeemer, and she slew him."[3] Just as Rahab and Ruth, an unknown woman becomes known and, in Jael's case, a hero for her actions.

The spiritual applications of Jael are clear. First, she was an *unknown woman* living a simple life of a nomad, dwelling in a tent. There was nothing in her résumé that made her a candidate to become a famous woman through just one act of faith. Christ was born in a stable instead of an inn; raised in the insignificant town of Nazareth instead of the holy city Jerusalem. He borrowed boats to preach from and a boy's lunch to feed a massive crowd in an outdoor picnic. Even His name in Hebrew, Yeshua, was Joshua, a very common name for young boys in His day. God took the common and made it uncommon, the simple became the glorious, and the plain became royalty. When you feel like a nobody, remember that God can take anybody and make them somebody because He is the I AM. The prayers of anybody who feels like a nobody will be answered when that person makes contact with God—the greatest somebody in the universe.

As a married woman, Jael knew what she wanted and didn't want in her house. At first she welcomed Sisera, but once he crossed the threshold into her dwelling, Jael desired to rid her home and Israel of this commander who sought the destruction of the Hebrew people. There are things you might put up with outside that you refuse to put up with inside; outside may affect others, but inside affects you. At times a dad will permit something in the house that a wife and mother knows has no business being on the property. Mothers and wives must become aggressive in resisting dangerous possibilities lurking in the darkness. There are times when a mama needs to get aggressive; take your spiritual broom and do a housecleaning.

This woman used tools in her home as weapons to tack the oppressor to the ground. Have you ever said to God, "If I only had the money I could do this..." "If I only had the right connections, I could do that..." "If I only had the right education, I could accomplish this..."? The simple fact is, all you need is the right faith and you can do the impossible. Often the residing resources within us are all the tools, resources, and weapons needed to defeat the adversary and move on to the next victory.

As far back as the Old Testament, a woman does not fight like a man. When the judge Deborah began sending messengers to the tribal leader to unite for war, most of the men were hesitant to join her. She brought Barak onto the team and instructed him to organize two tribes, Zebulun and Naphtali, into a war unit. The other tribes, Reuben, Dan, Gad, and Asher remained in their places and never went to war (Judg. 5:16–17). Some suggest these tribal clans didn't believe God would give a woman (Deborah) the victory in a war!

However, a woman does not fight like a man! The ancient

men going to war required swords, spears, helmets, shields, and any other form of protection. Neither Deborah nor Jael used any weapon or protection, as they fought with their minds (strategy) and with their spirits. David refused to wear Saul's armor and fought only with a sling and five stones (1 Sam. 17:40). In the David and Goliath encounter, and in the Deborah and Jael victory, it was not about weapons but about acts of obedience and the anointing. The anointing is a divine energy of enablement that breaks yokes, melts chains, and attacks the head or the source of the conflict. Be a Jael and nail the enemies of addiction, bondage, fear, unforgiveness, and unbelief in the head.

Mothers in Zion

In the poetic prose of Deborah she identifies herself as "a mother in Israel" (Judg. 5:7). This is a term used in some churches, identifying the senior women as Mothers in Zion. In the early days of some denominations the older women in the church were greatly honored with this title. These women of faith were at times widowed, having raised children now grown but often living in different states. Being retired from work with free time, their remaining days were spent as prayer warriors and volunteering in the church. They were sought out for their wisdom, as many years had provided them with life experiences that could save the younger women from heartache if they followed the wise paths of those who had gone before them.

In our own ministry we have a precious woman who is, at this time, eighty-six years of age. She is in good health and has a sharp mind and spirit. She hosts Bible studies in her home every second Wednesday, with forty to as many as sixty people attending. A few years ago she had twelve grown men living on her property, all men who had come out of prison. She spent time teaching them the Bible, praying with them, and at times disciplining them for their actions.

She was often asked, "Did you ever feel threatened or fearful, or was anything ever taken from your house?" The answer was "No." She replied, "Some of these men never had a spiritual parent in their life, and some had no mother or grandmother to direct them in right paths. They viewed me as their mother or grandmother and always treated me with respect, because if you do what is right with people, and they know your heart, they will give respect if you will show respect." She is now unable to house and teach these men, but she still has great zeal for God.

One of the greatest Mothers in Zion I have ever known is our beloved chief intercessor, Bea Ogle, from Pulaski, Virginia. She attends the Bob White Boulevard Church of God and first heard me speak at that church in 1980 as a young teenage minister. It was in 1981 that the Holy Spirit placed a burden upon her to consistently pray for me and the Voice of Evangelism ministry. She did this for many years, until during one season of prayer the Holy Spirit impressed upon her to raise up a prayer team of women called the Daughters of Rachel. The cry of Rachel was, "Give me children, or else I die" (Gen. 30:1). The goal of this prayer team was to pray for me and my family, for our health, protection, and strength to perform God's will, and to intercede for spiritual results, including for new babes in Christ to be spiritually birthed through the ministry. Through Bea's leadership, in thirty years she raised up more than sixteen hundred praying women, including state leaders, who have undergirded us in prayer.

Aunt Bea, as she is affectionately called by my family, staff, and the Daughters of Rachel prayer team, was never physically able to have natural children. She and her husband, Elroy, could never conceive a child. Years ago I told her that had she conceived a family of natural children, she would have never had the free time to spend hours in intercession, as today she would be caring for grandchildren. However, her "children" became all of the women intercessors who consider her a "spiritual and godly mother," who is greatly beloved by all who know her. Only heaven knows how many times her prayers prevented danger or even a premature death to myself, my family, or others connected with the ministry.

In the early 1990s I recall taking a team of eight individuals to Bulgaria for an evangelistic outreach. Our plane arrived late in Europe, and we missed the flight into Bulgaria. The team ended up flying to Rome, Italy, in hopes of connecting a later flight into Bulgaria, ministering on the weekend in the huge hall in Sofia. I didn't understand the reason for the delay and was quite upset that we had already missed several opportunities to minister in cities where the gospel had not been publicly presented due to forty years of Communist control, including a city predominant with Muslims in the south.

While in Rome I contacted my wife, Pam, to call Aunt Bea to pray for us to make it to Bulgaria. Bea told Pam that while I was on the plane she had a vision of me lying on what appeared to be an ambulance-type cot, with cuts all over my body from some type of glass that had cut me. She began praying for protection from whatever *accident* or attack was set in my path.

I, along with one ministry colleague, finally booked a flight from Rome to Sofia, Bulgaria. After meeting with the main bishop who was directing the services, I was informed that in the first city we were scheduled to minister—the one that we missed—a radical group, possibly terrorists, blew up a power plant, causing glass in windows to blow out and land on the street. The incident occurred at the same time we would have been ministering in an outdoor meeting, in the same city near the site of the explosion. We also learned that the same car we would have been in, driving to and from the city, had two tires blow out the same day we would have been traveling. Missing the plane was actually the Lord's protection. The intercession of a woman, Bea Ogle, prayed us out of danger's way.

The Story of Judith

There are numerous books that are non-canonical, that is they are not considered divinely inspired and are not in the present Protestant canon of Scripture. Such is the Book of Judith. This unusual story is included in the Septuagint and in the Catholic and Eastern Orthodox Old Testaments and was read by Clement of Rome, but other fathers placed it in the category of the Apocrypha. Jerome spoke of Judith as an example of a holy widow and a type of the church.[4] Many scholars consider the narrative more of a parable instead of an actual historical narrative. During the Middle Ages, it became customary for a Hebrew midrashic variant of the Judith story to be read on the Shabbat of Hanukkah.[5] The Book of Judith tells a story of a woman who became a heroine for defeating an enemy of Israel.

In the narrative a widowed Jewish woman named Judith is frustrated with her people for not trusting God to deliver them from the hands of their enemies. She and her maid travel into the enemy's camp, meeting a general named Holofernes, who was sent by the King of Nineveh to subdue the Jews. Judith worked her way into gaining the trust of the enemy by posing as an informer to expose important information about the Israelites. Gaining his confidence, Judith enters the tent while the general is in a drunken condition, making her move and beheading him, bringing his head back to show to the fearful Israelites. She becomes a national heroine, remaining unmarried all her days (Judith 8–16). Thus Israel was delivered by the hand of a woman—a steady theme in the book (Judith 8:33; 9:9; 12:4; 15:10).

In the stories of Deborah and Judith, the main area of the battle is near or on the plains of Esdraelon, better known as the Valley of Armageddon. The brook Kishon, where Sisera's nine hundred chariots were destroyed (Judg. 5:21), runs through this prophetic valley. It is the same valley where the final *Mother of all Battles*, the Battle of Armageddon will occur (Rev. 16:16). The Kishon is also the river where Elijah slaughtered the false prophets of Baal (1 Kings 18:40). This valley and river are the site of numerous prophetic events that connect with Israel's deliverance.

Both Jael and Judith stopped the enemy by going after the *head* of the enemy. The spiritual principle of the authority of the head is understood in both the kingdom of God and the kingdom of darkness. The wife of Ahab, Jezebel, threatened to behead Elijah after he slew her false prophets (1 Kings 19), and in the New Testament, the "spirit of Jezebel" manifested when the daughter of Herodias lewdly danced before Herod, stirring his passion. After vowing to grant her whatever she desired, her mother sent word asking for the *head* of John the Baptist on a silver platter (Matt. 14:3–11). The spirit of Jezebel always goes after the person who clashes with her wicked ways by attacking the head, or spiritual authority, since when the shepherd or spiritual head is *smitten*, the sheep will scatter (Mark 14:27).

The same spiritual principle operates in God's kingdom. If believers can discover the head or the *root* of a spiritual conflict and attack the adversary at the core source of the battle, then we can reposition ourselves from the victim to the victor. Crush the head and the enemy will scatter. Jael took a nail and nailed the head of her enemy to the earth. With a hammer and a nail the enemy was conquered (Judg. 5:24–27). Generations later the Roman soldiers took a hammer and nails thinking they were ridding the earth of the scourge of Christ. However, what they intended to be the end was only the beginning of a new redemptive covenant. With a hammer and nails the blood released from Christ became the weapon that crushed the head of the serpent (Gen. 3:15).

Nail It in the Head

The phrase "hit the nail on the head" is used figuratively when a person does something right in an effective and efficient manner. It can also mean to get to the precise point in a matter. Believers must discern the root causes of spiritual and mental conflicts by hitting the nail on the head or going after the root causes instead of focusing on the surface circumstances. Jael destroyed the authority of Israel's enemy with a hammer and nail, which stopped the wicked *thinking* of Sisera and his *mouth* from ever boasting again.

The adversary is after your mind—your head. When Delilah was paid to discover the secret of Samson's strength, she took his seven locks of hair and attached them with a *pin* to a loom (Judg. 16:14). The loom normally held yarn required to weave together a garment. The imagery here is how the enemy weaves your life with destructive people and negative circumstances, hoping to *pin you* into a hopeless situation—just as Delilah used a loom and a pin, thinking she could control Samson. She and the Philistines wanted the secret of Samson's strength because his strongman demonstrations—burning down fields and ripping gates off the city—were destroying the Philistine properties.

The enemy is a master of hiding the root causes of personal struggles, causing us to focus on the surface issues and preventing us from finding the undercurrent that is rocking the ship. During the past several years, my wife and I have been involved in the lives of many women through the Women of Hope rehab ministry—for women who have battled various narcotic addictions. I used to believe that addictions were rooted in a person's desire to get *high* or just to be in the *in crowd*. These may be two surface reasons, but they are not the root. When digging deep into the well of the soul, the root cause is hurt from the past, which includes physical and verbal abuse, and the narcotics, alcohol, and drugs are attempts to cover the pain and hurt and to dull the senses so a woman can avoid dealing with the issues or people that have wounded them. If a person only deals with the surface, then the underlying cause goes ignored, and when the opportunity and occasion arises, the addict will be right back into the addiction. This is why counseling is an important element in recovery; removing the layers of lies people have believed will put a nail in the head of deception.

Jeremiah wrote:

> See, I have this day set you over the nations and over the
> kingdoms,
> To root out and to pull down,
> To destroy and to throw down,
> To build and to plant.
> —JEREMIAH 1:10

Old roots must be pulled out and strongholds pulled down to plant the good seed of the Word of God that will rebuild, planting a tree of righteousness to produce fruit.

One of the major issues facing a generation of parents is the rebellion in their children. Parents are continually attempting to discern the source of their kids' conflict. The common observation is, "They are getting with the wrong crowd and being influenced by the wrong people." Wrong people bring wrong influence. However, the root reason for rebelling against parental authority is often internal family conflicts, including divorce within the home. Rebellion is the visible *fruit* of a *root of bitterness* caused by the infighting at home and the fact that one of the biological parents is missing. The Hebrew word *rebellion* is *meri*, and is also a word for bitter or bitterness. When struggling with your children who are in rebellion, you must search for the head, the true source stirring the emotion of resistance to your authority, and deal with the root and not just the fruit. The *nail of prayer* must be focused on the head of the conflict—not a person per se, but the agitating force causing the negative circumstance.

The symbol for Satan is a serpent (Gen. 3:13; Rev. 20:1). Snakes fall into two categories: poisonous and nonpoisonous. During my lifetime, I have accidently come across various snakes and have never, and I mean never, taken the time to stop and check out the type of head and detailed colors of these subtle creatures. My reaction is to run as fast as I can in the opposite direction, to avoid being a taste test or appetizer for the fangs of these reptiles. The danger of any venomous serpent is in its *mouth*—which is located in its *head*.

Years ago I saw a man in the mountains of Virginia run over a dangerous rattlesnake. He got out of his vehicle, took a stick and moved the snake from its dying spot. We later returned to see the remains of this beast of the woods, only to discover it had crawled away! I learned that the head of a snake can be removed from its body, but it is able to discharge venom up to two hours. However, the only way of slaying a venomous serpent is to go after its head, as the danger is in the head and the mouth. Men seek to take out venomous snakes by striking their heads, but serpents hide low to bite the heels of men. As stated with the tribe of Dan, when the snake bites the horse on the heels, the rider will fall backward (Gen. 49:17). Snakes conceal themselves and adapt to their surroundings. If we don't watch and pray, we could be stricken while walking in dangerous territory.

The Skin of the Serpent

The serpent emblem is often used in biblical narratives. Moses's rod was cast down before Pharaoh's magicians, becoming a serpent and later changing back into a rod (Exod. 7:9–12). After being bitten by burning serpents in the wilderness, Moses set a brass serpent on a pole. When those poisoned by the fangs of the vipers looked to the brass serpent, they were cured (Num. 21:8–9). The rod of Moses was a symbol of the Tree of Life, and the brass snake on the pole was a symbol of Christ on the cross (John 3:14–15). The serpent promises that through sinning a person will enjoy life but sin leads to death. The Messiah took the sins of the world and through death gives life.

To the Egyptians this *serpent magic* that Moses performed was duplicated by their own magicians, Jannes and Jambres (2 Tim. 3:8). However, Moses's serpent swallowed the two rods of the magicians, just as Christ swallowed death and hell through His resurrection. The serpent also has the ability to shed its skin, to renew itself by removing the old and putting on the new. The staff of Moses was a dead tree branch that suddenly became alive and reverted back to a rod. The snake shedding its old skin and growing a new one holds a power application when in spiritual conflict.

In a specific area of your life where you struggled and have gained total freedom, the adversary, the old serpent (Rev. 9:12), will shed his old skin to put on new—or attempt to induce a new type of bondage, addiction, or challenge to your life. He's the same old snake with a new look; the same old enemy but a fresh touch, brighter colors, more appealing now than in the past. As an example, in earlier days any printed magazines with pornography were wrapped in brown paper and hidden under a counter. Then the snake changed his skin and brought the magazines into racks covered with brown wrappers. This became *old*, and it was time for a *new* strategy, as some men didn't want to be seen in a store purchasing these types of publications. The serpent put on a new outfit and brought the porno into the home on cable. Now the slithering serpent has a new look and has made images available in a computer and a phone. The availability moved from a store to the home. The clash between two kingdoms—God's and Satan's—is in the home.

Jael represents the woman who discerns that what is in her tent (house) is an enemy and must be dealt with. Paul makes it clear that our struggle is not against "flesh and blood," but against different levels and types of wicked spirits: principalities, powers, rulers of darkness, and wicked spirits in high places (Eph. 6:12).

The enemy is limited if he's on the outside, but he is empowered if he gets on the inside. If Satan ever wants to destroy a person, he will send a person to you as his assignment against you. There is a woman somewhere who is designed to destroy every man of God, and a man somewhere being set up by the adversary to wreck the ministry of every woman of God. For every marriage, somewhere there is a coworker who can become the tool for interrupting and eventually destroying a family unit. Your own sons and daughters are under the scope of other youth who could target them, poisoning them toward a life of addiction or sexual perversion.

Satan's greatest threat is godly people, and his greatest tools are unrighteous people. Without a person, demonic agents have no voice to speak, no hands to work, and no feet to follow paths of iniquity. Look at Job. Once Satan entered Job's world, nomadic tribes of Chaldeans and Sabeans stole his animals, his wife wanted him to "curse" God and die, and his friends showed up and gave their theological opinions, which discouraged the ex-millionaire even more (Job 1–5).

The internal strategy of people's influence is simple: its goal is to break down a person's willpower to be weakened and aligned to the will of the adversary. Sin occurs when the will to do right is exchanged for the choice of being disobedient. Willful and premeditated sin is the worst type, as it differs from falling into a sin under intense pressure. Willful repeating of sin without repenting of sins will place layers of hardness on the heart and reasoning of the person. This is when the conscience becomes seared (1 Tim. 4:2), and the person is unable to hear the voice and feel the warmth of the Holy Spirit's conviction. The *conscience* is the voice of the human spirit, and *conviction* is the voice of the Holy Spirit. A person who has never encountered the Holy Spirit is still given a conscience to discern right and wrong, justice and injustice, good and evil in the earth. There is a progression in the *searing* process.

I can remember as a young teenager how offended my spirit would become when I would hear profanity. I had no desire to fellowship with a person in spiritual darkness as we had nothing in common. I recall a minister who purchased satellite time on television, who was a brilliant teacher and had written Sunday school literature for one of the major Pentecostal denominations. However, he would sit in a chair wearing a hat, smoking a huge cigar, and at times throw a dart at a large map and wherever it landed, demand someone from that town or city to send him an offering or he would quit teaching until the phone rang. I recall the first time I saw him how grieved I was that people would think this is what a minister is like and what ministry is about. However, the more some people watched him, the more they considered him *entertaining*.

If Satan's main tool is unrighteous and carnal people, then his major weapon is ignorance through darkness. Spiritual darkness is not just a mental condition but it is also a spiritual position. Spiritual darkness is not removed by mind over matter or confessing the right combinations. For example, the US government spent millions of dollars on an anti-drug campaign with a three-word theme, "Just say no," speaking of saying no to drugs. When a person has no desire to do drugs, saying no is as easy as refusing to drive to California from Atlanta nonstop both ways— the idea or the *temptation* is not even on the charts. However, it is difficult to say no if your mind and body are screaming yes. All of the "no, no, noes" with your mouth will become void when they are not in your heart.

The mind is always attacked first, as the thoughts in the mind control the body and the spirit, for as a man "thinks in his heart, so is he" (Prov. 23:7). We are warned in Scripture not to lose faith in our minds (Col. 1:23), for weariness in the mind removes the hedges of defense and can increase the level of temptation.

Giving Away Our Spiritual Authority

The enemy is not stealing the authority of the church; *believers are giving it away by default.* The way battles are lost is by passively accepting what comes your way and refusing to resist. One great danger for a believer is to turn spiritual authority into a formula, equating the process of a formula to the power behind authority.

At Ephesus Paul demonstrated great signs and wonders, confirming the Word among the people. Paul's spiritual authority was demonstrated when pieces of cloth from his body were prayed over and given to the sick and demon possessed. Instantly the sick were cured, and the possessed were released from demonic control (Acts 19:11–12). A group of seven *professional* Jewish exorcists, all sons of a chief priest named Sceva, were so impressed with Paul they found a demon-possessed man and spoke over him the *formula* Paul used. Their words were, "In the name of the Jesus whom Paul preaches, I command you to come out." The demoniac stared them down and replied, "Jesus I know, and Paul I know about, but who are you?"

41

The man lunged for the seven men, ripping off their clothes and sending them streaking into the streets (Acts 19:13–16, NIV).

They had no real spiritual authority but used a formula—the name of Jesus—without true faith. The demon knew Jesus and Paul but none of these other men (v. 15). This story reveals that what we confess with our mouths is only words unless it is found first in our hearts—"out of the abundance of the heart the mouth speaks" (Matt. 12:34). If we anoint someone with oil in the name of the Lord and pray a prayer *without faith*, we have merely exercised a formula without faith (see James 5:14). If we worship with words from our lips in a public setting but our hearts are in another place, then our worship is in vain (Matt. 15:9).

Four Spiritual Tools
Every Mother Should Use

When God established His moral, judicial, and spiritual laws and statutes in the Torah, He blessed the wombs and the children that would be birthed through the women who received His Word. We read, "And He will love you and bless you and multiply you; He will also bless the fruit of your womb" (Deut. 7:13), and "You shall be blessed above all peoples; there shall not be a male or female barren among you" (v. 14). The blessing was passed to the seed of the righteous; "May the LORD give you increase more and more, you and your children" (Ps. 115:14). Children should never be a burden to the mother who birthed them, as they are called "a heritage from the LORD, the fruit of the womb is a reward" (Ps. 127:3). The word *heritage* in Hebrew is *nachalah,* and can refer to an inheritance or an heirloom that is passed on after the death of one owning an estate. When your children birth their children, then your name, family history, and legacy are passed on as your children's spiritual inheritance.

To protect the heritage in your bloodline will often require spiritual warfare—holding on to God's promises and praying away the demonic forces and wrong soul ties that are harassing your children. There are four things every mother or soon-to-be mother should establish and know.

The promises of God for family blessing

The first tool every woman should be familiar with is *the promises* of God designed for family blessings, such as the scriptures listed above in the first paragraph of this section. When an earthquake broke the foundation and prison bars in a Roman jail, the jailer was preparing to commit suicide, and Paul stopped him. He and his family were unconverted souls. A promise was given to him that "You will be saved, you and your household" (Acts 16:31). When Cornelius and his family heard Peter's message, the Holy Spirit fell upon them and the entire house was baptized in the Holy Spirit (Acts 10:44–46). At Corinth in Greece, a ruler of the local synagogue named Crispus believed on Christ along with his entire house (Acts 18:8). In the house of Philip his four virgin daughters were considered prophetesses—thus his house was a house of believers (Acts 21:8–9). One disciple of the Lord named Stephanas was a father whose entire house were believers and had devoted themselves to the ministry of the saints (1 Cor. 16:15). Every mother and father must be totally convinced without wavering that it is the will of God to save their entire house. The reason God chose Abraham is He knew his faith would be passed on from generation to generation. We read:

> For I have known him, in order that he may command his children and his household after him, that they keep the way

of the LORD, to do righteousness and justice, that the LORD may bring to Abraham what He has spoken to him.

—GENESIS 18:19

When claiming the promise of full family salvation, the seeker in prayer should take on the spirit of Abraham and in prayer commit to raising his or her children in the ways of the Lord.

Your spoken words

The second tool is understanding that your spoken words must become *vertical prayers* to God and *horizontal confessions* on earth. Christ taught the principle of speaking to mountains and commanding them to be removed. He taught, "Whatever things you ask when you pray, believe that you receive them, and you will have them" (Mark 11:22–24). Speaking a blessing is so significant that God instructed the high priest to lift his hands and speak these words over the people:

> The LORD bless you and keep you;
> The LORD make His face shine upon you,
> And be gracious to you;
> The LORD lift up His countenance upon you,
> And give you peace.
>
> —NUMBERS 6:24–26

Whatever words we speak toward heaven must be echoed and agreed with on earth. When we *claim* a promise in prayer, later speaking contrary to what we pray could abort the spiritual progress we are making. When Israel departed from Egypt, while living in tents in the wilderness they began speaking contrary to God's promises in the privacy of the dwellings, complaining and griping about their discomfort. God overheard their conversation (murmuring) in their tents (Deut. 1:27) and blocked their promise for forty years, preventing the Egypt generation from inheriting their land. Words either please or displease God; we should pray, "Let the words of my mouth...be acceptable in Your sight, O Lord" (Ps. 19:14).

This is an area requiring continual discipline if your family's DNA or nature is to be negative, opinionated, and outspoken. We pray in faith yet converse to others in unbelief. The words that are the enemies of faith are *if* and *maybe*. Have you ever said, "If God ever does this..." or "If he (or she) ever comes to the Lord..."? Perhaps you have said, "If they will ever get their life together *maybe* things will change." Depending on how it is used, *if* implies uncertainty: "I will be there *if* nothing happens." That is not a firm commitment but an uncertain possibility. We seldom pray with an "if" because we pray the scriptural promises, which are "Yes" and "Amen" (2 Cor. 1:20). The "if" usually follows the *waiting period* from the time of our prayer to the moment of the answer. If the answer is delayed, we assume, "Well, maybe it's not the will of God" or "Maybe God has another plan."

Years ago I sensed the Holy Spirit pricking my heart when after prayer I would speak of the answer with terms of *if* and *maybe*. Instead of saying, "*If* they ever come to know the Lord," I was impressed to say, "*When* they receive the Lord," and "When it happens..." *When* indicates a *set moment that will come*: "When you get here." "When the package arrives." "When do you want to go and eat?" Your *if* should become a *when*, and your *maybe* must become a *certainty*. The word of faith is both in our *mouths* and in our *hearts* (Rom. 10:8). Let your words after you pray agree with the words you spoke when you prayed.

Defy the devil

The third spiritual tool you must understand is the *tenacity to defy the devil* that is destroying your bloodline. Growing up in church, there were times I felt that believers had more faith in the trouble the devil could send than in the blessing God could provide! On several occasions, when a strong man or woman of faith would declare we had spiritual authority and should resist and rebuke Satan, a well-meaning but battle-worn saint would warn, "Better be careful…the devil will hear that and attack you," or "You are going to make the devil angry if you keep speaking against his kingdom." After years of ministry I can respond to these two warnings with these observations. First, the enemy will attack you, whether you provoke him or not. Testing and temptation are a part of living on a cursed planet where the "god of this age" (2 Cor. 4:4) dominates the culture. As far as Satan's anger, he has always been angry, and at the time of the end his anger reaches a climax just before he is bound in the abyss for a thousand years (Rev. 12:12). There are two statements the Holy Spirit gave me that fit in this section. First, *the anger of Satan can never be greater than the love of God!* Second, *there is no battle big enough that God has not already planned a victorious outcome for you.* It was Christ who promised you authority over all the powers of the enemy and promised that nothing (from the kingdom of darkness) would by any means harm you (Luke 10:19). Your boldness (tenacity) to rebuke the enemy, commanding him to get his hands off your children and family, rest in your position in Christ, as you are using His name, His Spirit, His authority, and His Word.

Access to angelic assistance

A fourth tool and weapon of warfare is the believer's ability to gain *access to angelic assistance.* In Hebrews 1:13–14 the "ministering spirits" refer to angelic messengers assigned to minister to those who will inherit salvation. In the early church there were some who were enamored with angels, to the point of angel worship, which should never occur, as angels are assigned to worship

God and Christ alone. (See Revelation 5:11–12.) However, throughout the Bible angels assisted men and women in bringing revelation, connecting covenant believers together (Acts 10), announcing birth (Luke 1), and ministering strength (Luke 22:43). Angels are invisible to the human eye, but at times can manifest in the form of a human. When you become weary in well doing, or sense the heat from the fire, never be hesitant to ask for the supernatural assistance of angels.

Clearly the tools are in your hands. With the *faith* of Rahab, the *strategies* of Deborah, and the *zeal* of Jael and Judith, the adversary is in trouble when a woman of God finds her hot spot that's burning holes in heaven from her prayer closet as she focuses her energy toward one assignment.

CHAPTER 4

RELEASING A FIRSTFRUIT FAMILY BLESSING

T O UNDERSTAND WHY SUCH A LEVEL OF FAVOR WAS imparted to Rahab and Ruth, one must understand the spiritual principles of the law of firstfruits. The word *firstfruits* in Hebrew is *bikkurim*, and refers to the first in a family, first among animals, first ripened grains, and fruit on trees. Israel was instructed to participate in seven festivals or convocations, with three merging in succession in the spring—Passover, Unleavened Bread, and Firstfruits. Prior to the barley harvest, which was in full swing when Ruth and Naomi entered Bethlehem (Ruth 1:22), the high priest would enter the field to find the first ripened barley, marking and cutting the section with a sickle, presenting them to God at the tabernacle and later at the temple in Jerusalem. Each day for forty-nine consecutive days the priest took a handful of grain, called *counting the omer*, which climaxed on the fiftieth day, which introduced the fourth great festival, Pentecost. Firstfruits required certain rituals and activities.

This firstfruits principle includes a law for the firstborn male sons. The laws of the firstborn of men, grains, and fruits are recorded in Exodus.

1. Exodus 13:2 (KJV)—"Sanctify unto me all the firstborn, whatsoever openeth the womb among the children of Israel, both of man and of beast."

2. Exodus 13:15—Sanctify to the Lord all males that open the womb, the firstborn of Israel.

3. Exodus 22:29—Offer the first ripened produce and juices, and the firstborn of your sons to the Lord.

4. Exodus 34:20—All your firstborn sons you shall redeem with a lamb, none shall appear before the Lord empty-handed.

God's original plan was for all firstborn Hebrew sons to be set aside for the tabernacle priesthood (Num. 3:13). However, after the Israelites, through Aaron's hands, melted gold and molded the golden calf, followed by Moses demanding the Levites to slay the idolaters, God separated the tribe of Levi unto Himself to serve as the priests of the tabernacle and the temple:

> And you shall take the Levites for Me—I am the LORD—instead of all the firstborn among the children of Israel, and the livestock of the Levites instead of all the firstborn among the livestock of the children of Israel.
> —NUMBERS 3:41

> For all the firstborn among the children of Israel are Mine, both man and beast; on the day that I struck all the firstborn

in the land of Egypt I sanctified them to Myself. I have taken the Levites instead of all the firstborn of the children of Israel. And I have given the Levites as a gift to Aaron and his sons from among the children of Israel, to do the work for the children of Israel in the tabernacle of meeting, and to make atonement for the children of Israel, that there be no plague among the children of Israel when the children of Israel come near the sanctuary.

—Numbers 8:17–19

The Levites were called out above the other eleven tribes, but Israel as a whole was considered God's chosen nation. Why did the Hebrews attract God's attention and affection above all tribes or nations? The answer is that Israel was the first and only nation that was called God's "firstborn"—a nation whose birth was personally designed by the Almighty, and the only nation that was *founded* and *maintained* by a one-on-one covenant with God. The revelation of Israel's position with God was revealed to Pharaoh:

Then you shall say to Pharaoh, "Thus says the Lord: 'Israel is My son, My firstborn. So I say to you, let My son go that he may serve Me. But if you refuse to let him go, indeed I will kill your son, your firstborn.'"

—Exodus 4:22–23

There were originally seventy nations that God separated after the Flood, and seventy souls came out of the loins of Jacob (Exod. 1:5). However, God chose one man, Abraham, to possess one land, Canaan Land, to bring forth one people, the Hebrews, and birth one true religion with the one true God. All nations would be blessed because of God's firstborn son, Israel. The Hebrew nation is the firstfruits of God's increase, as God blessed them to be a blessing to the entire world.

I will make you a great nation;
I will bless you
And make your name great;
And you shall be a blessing.
I will bless those who bless you,
And I will curse him who curses you;
And in you all the families of the earth shall be blessed.

—GENESIS 12:2–3

Jerusalem—God's Home Away from Home

Israel is God's chosen nation, with Jerusalem His chosen city. Jerusalem is *God's home away from home*, or His miniature heaven on earth, and it was the center of spiritual activity in the days of Abraham and Melchizedek—the first king and priest to God. At that time the city was called Salem (Gen. 14:18). Abraham had divine revelation that there, in the mountains of Moriah, a future lamb would be seen, as God Himself would initiate a redemptive covenant (Gen. 22:8, 14). For centuries scholars have pondered why, with all the land on this planet, God would select as His dwelling the mountains of Jerusalem (Ps. 125:2). The speculation is endless. However, the city is believed to be located in the center of the nations (Ezek. 5:5).

Jerusalem's special bond with God also connects with David. In Psalms 89 God called David "one chosen from the people" (v. 19). God made David his firstborn and highest of the kings of the earth (v. 27). Israel's first king, Saul, was from the tribe of Benjamin, but David was from the tribe of Judah. The promise to inherit Jerusalem was given to the descendants of David. A title given to the Messiah is the "Son of David"; for God has promised to preserve David's seed forever (Ezek. 37:24–25; Ps. 89:3).

Rahab—Israel's Firstfruits

The timing of the conquest of Jericho was in the spring during the three main spring festivals: Passover, Unleavened Bread, and Firstfruits. We know this by observing details in the Book of Joshua. The Hebrews departed from Egypt at Passover and entered the Promised Land during Passover, at the end of forty years. We read:

> Now the children of Israel camped in Gilgal, and kept the Passover on the fourteenth day of the month at twilight on the plains of Jericho. And they ate of the produce of the land on the day after the Passover, unleavened bread and parched grain, on the very same day. Then the manna ceased on the day after they had eaten the produce of the land; and the children of Israel no longer had manna, but they ate the food of the land of Canaan that year.
>
> —JOSHUA 5:10–12

Joshua had circumcised the men born in the wilderness, since circumcision was the sign of the Abrahamic covenant between the Hebrew males and God (Josh. 5:8). After the mass circumcision, the head angel of God's heavenly armies ("captain of the LORD's hosts," KJV), revealed the conquest strategy to Joshua—to march around the city for six days, and on the seventh day blow the trumpets and shout (Josh. 6:1–5). These six days would fall in line with the weeklong observation of firstfruits, when Israel offered the first ripened barley before the Lord.

This explains why God gave instruction that everything inside of Jericho was to be given, 100 percent, to the tabernacle of the Lord. In no other city after Jericho did God demand a percentage of the war spoil. Jericho was the first Canaanite city to be captured and reclaimed by Israel, and the "first" belongs to the Lord. If the people stored all the gold, silver, brass, and other spoils from Jericho in the house of God, then the soldiers could keep the items captured from the other cities. If, however, they refused to follow this law of firstfruits, a curse would follow Israel, and they would cease to maintain the ability to conquer other cities. This is why when at Jericho Achan withheld the precious metals and Babylonian garment, all of Israel suffered from one man's disobedience. Joshua's penalty for Achan's disobedience was severe—a death penalty by stoning (Josh. 7). Joshua had spent forty years living in a desert because of the sin of unbelief from two spies, and this military commander and spiritual leader had no desire to be forced back into a dry wilderness, thus he severely judged the sin, releasing God's favor back upon the army.

Releasing the firstfruits to God brought a special blessing upon the Israelite's house. This is revealed by Ezekiel:

> The best of all firstfruits of any kind, and every sacrifice of any kind from all your sacrifices, shall be the priest's; also you shall give to the priest the first of your ground meal, to cause a blessing to rest on your house.
>
> —EZEKIEL 44:30

This was the spiritual principle guiding Rahab's own blessings. In the narrative Joshua was slightly over eighty years of age, and his companion Caleb was about eighty-five when both men directed the most unusual military conquest in history, the taking of Jericho, followed by about thirty-one other Canaanite cities (Josh. 21). The inhabitants of Jericho had one of three options:

1. Get up, get out, and leave the city unoccupied

2. Give up peacefully and allow Israel to take the spoil for the tabernacle

3. Resist the Hebrew army and experience a war

Forty years earlier Rahab had heard of the Hebrew God and His miraculous feats. Jericho was the main city on a trade route, located near the Jordan River with an oasis and a spring, providing fresh water for caravans. Across the Jordan was Edom and Moab. God had opened the Red Sea, and the Hebrews slew Og and Sihon, two giant men with armies, and had subdued their enemies in Moab and Bashan. During those forty years, travelers had stopped by the inn of Jericho and told stunning stories, warning that Israel would eventually seize the land of Canaan. These stories terrified the people of the city, and Rahab knew that in time she would need to make a decision on whose side she would stand: with the people of Jericho or with the God of the Hebrews.

Using Secret Strategies

Different warfare requires different strategies. When preparing for this battle, Joshua may have recalled a terrible crisis, forty years prior, when he and Caleb returned with ten other spies and those ten men talked themselves into unbelief, spreading fear like a plague to all Israel, painting an image of weakness and helplessness in taking over the Promised Land from giants and walled cities. Moses had publicly commissioned these twelve men to bring back a report—and after forty days ten of them gave an "evil report" (Num. 13:32, KJV). Perhaps this is why Joshua sent two spies in and did so without announcing his plans to anyone. In the event these two spies came back with a negative attitude, no one but Joshua would know because Joshua knew he did not have another forty years to go back into the wilderness because of someone's unbelief.

Joshua understood that unbelief can stop cold the progression of God's blessings. In the Scripture the Lord provides us with what I have termed *faith tools* to help us release our faith at a particular moment. For example, a *faith tool* of the doctrine of "laying on of hands" (Heb. 6:2). This sacred ritual was used in both testaments. The high priest (or elders) would lay his hands upon the sacrifices, symbolically transferring the sins of the people to the animal (Lev. 4:15; 16:21). This *faith tool* was used by Moses when he and others would lay their hands on others to transfer wisdom or anointing (Deut. 34:9). In the New Testament this method was used to impart healing, the Holy Spirit baptism, the setting apart of men for the office of bishop, and for exorcisms (Acts 19:6; 28:8; 1 Tim. 4:14). When an anointed minister lays hands upon individuals and prays for their personal needs, that moment is when faith is to be released and mixed with the anointing. It is a *faith moment*, for when faith mingles with the unction of the Spirit great results occur.

One of the most unique New Testament faith tools was the *cloths* of Paul, taken from his body and placed on the sick and demonic possessed. There is no inherent power or authority in a piece of cotton or linen cloth, but an act of faith moved the hand of God for His intervention.

There have been many occasions when an unsaved family member or a relative locked in a prison of bondage or chained with spiritual rebellion would not, on their own, read a Bible, or attend church or a prayer meeting. This passive attitude that expresses no interest in spiritual matters often discourages concerned family members and leaves them with a "what can I do" feeling. Over the years I have encouraged men and women to pray over prayer cloths or other objects that the unsaved person would be in contact with, or to place a prayer cloth under the bed of the unsaved individual, as a *secret weapon*. This cloth marks the spot for an expected visitation from the Holy Spirit to bring deliverance to the one being prayed for.

The fact that Rahab the town prostitute could turn from her sinful lifestyle, converting to God and bringing forth such an amazing historical narrative, and a genealogy that is unmatched by any other Gentile woman outside of Ruth, reveals that there is no one with a negative past whom God cannot transform into a positive future.

When Transition Comes to Your House

The timing of the Jericho conquest is significant in connection with the conversion of Rahab and her house. It was the conclusion of forty years of dwelling in tents in the wilderness, and eating manna, the bread from heaven. The conquest began about one month after Moses's death, as Israel mourned Moses's departure for thirty days (Deut. 34:8). Four major transitions occurred at one time.

First, the pillar of cloud by day and the fire by night ceases. The desert heat in the day can be almost unbearable in the summer, and cooler at night during the winter months. God's supernatural cloud provided a shield from the sun, and the night fire allowed the people to move about after sunset with a light glowing above their camp and providing warmth in the cooler nights.

This represented a shifting in the atmosphere. Jericho was not the wilderness, but it was an oasis of palms. There was abundant grass along with fruit trees in the land, and the removal of the cloud and fire was a shifting in the heavens. Elijah endured a forty-two-month drought and saw a famine so severe people were dying. However, during intense intercession, the heavens shifted, and a cloud formed like a man's hand. This hand-cloud broke the drought and brought the rain (1 Kings 18:42–46). When God's hand begins moving in your famine and drought, the atmosphere will change. You can feel a breakthrough coming before it ever arrives.

Second, the manna ceased. The generation with Joshua had eaten manna, but now was the first generation in forty years to enjoy the grain from the land, as this was the season of the barley harvest, and the people "did eat the old corn of the land" (Josh. 5:11, KJV). The Hebrew word "corn" in the KJV is the Hebrew *abuwr*, which is only used of *stored grain*. There were grain fields in the area of Moab where they were camping before crossing the Jordan River. Israel may have raided the grain fields of their enemies while in the Moab region.

Believers often depend upon the prayers and support of others for many years, carrying them from one crisis to the other, always depending upon a family member or friend to provide their help or spiritual undergirding. Babies need bottle feeding, but adults need forks. There comes a time when God requires believers to *feed themselves* and go after their own spiritual food—reading and studying the Bible personally, praying alone, and worshipping by faith. Many animals, such as squirrels, can detect when winter is approaching and begin storing up their food for winter. It has been noted that if a winter is going to be long and harsh, the old-timers knew by the amount of acorns on the ground. God was providing for His creation by increasing the food supply before winter! When the manna from heaven ceased, there was none to collect in the fields.

Third, the young men had not been circumcised in the wilderness, and circumcision was the sign of the sons of Abraham and their covenant with God (Gen. 17:11). Joshua understood that if these young men went to battle, they had no covenant favor with God and thus could lose the war. Joshua took flint knives and circumcised all the young men over twenty who would be required to fight against the tribes in the Promised Land. This was very painful for older men.

Our circumcision today is not of the flesh but of the heart (Rom. 2:29). There are times we must pray for the Lord to *cut things* out of us that are hindering us. This cutting may be a transition from a place where we are stuck to a place where we will discover God's purpose—a new job, finding a new church, or cutting the ropes connecting you to negative friends, fleeing like Joseph did from the wife of Potiphar (Gen. 39:12).

The fourth transition was a visitation from the angel of the Lord. At the beginning of the Exodus, God informed Moses that an angel would remain in the cloud and the fire throughout their journey, preparing the way for them. This mysterious angel had the name of the Lord upon him, and if Israel sinned he would not forgive their iniquity (Exod. 23:20–23). When the cloud and pillar ceased, this angel came out of the cloud and was seen by Joshua as the "captain of the LORD's host" (Josh. 5:14–15).

Rahab, the Firstfruits

Rahab was unique as she was Israel's very *first convert* to the Hebrew God from the Promised Land itself. The law of firstfruits indicates that not only is the firstfruit blessed, but also the field from which it is harvested becomes blessed—the field being the land of Israel. Her faith spread to her family, and her deliverance from death was also passed to her bloodline. She eventually met and married a Hebrew, thus beginning her legacy as a woman of faith. Matthew speaks of her in his genealogical listings of the ancestors of Christ:

> And Salmon begot Boaz by Rahab, Boaz begot Obed by Ruth, Obed begot Jesse, and Jesse begot David the king. David the king begot Solomon by her who had been the wife of Uriah.
> —MATTHEW 1:5–6

Rahab began her spiritual legacy after converting and surviving the destruction of Jericho, and marrying Salmon. Since it is unlikely Joshua would have sent two *married* men to the house of the prostitute, some suggest Rahab married one of the two spies, which are unnamed in the narrative, but one may have been this man named Salmon. Rahab birthed a famous son named Boaz. This is the same Boaz who owned the fields of Bethlehem in the Book of Ruth, meaning that Boaz had inherited a huge land grant from his father, Salmon. The city of Jericho is located in the Jordan Valley at the base of the Judean Wilderness. Jericho is at the edge of the tribe of Judah, and Bethlehem was the main city of that tribe. Rahab and her husband settled in this region and obtained an inheritance that was passed to their famous son, mentioned in the Book of Ruth. Rahab was a Gentile convert, and the wife of her son, Boaz, was Ruth, a Moabite and also a Gentile converted to the God of Abraham.

Boaz and Ruth had a son named Obed, who after the death of Boaz would have inherited all of his parents' wheat and barley fields. As an infant Obed was the baby held in the arms of Naomi, the mother-in-law to Ruth, which brought her joy in her old age (Ruth 4:17). When Obed was married, his son was named Jesse, who also would inherit the same fields of his ancestors. This was the same Jesse who was the father of seven sons, including David. Thus, the fields where David watched sheep were the exact same pieces of land where David's great-grandmother and her husband settled after the conquests of the Promised Land.

One woman's decision to place a scarlet thread in her window would change the destiny of mankind, as this former prostitute is one of five women listed in the genealogies of Christ in Matthew chapter 1: Tamar (v. 3), Rahab (v. 5), Ruth (v. 5), Bathsheba (v. 6), and Mary (v. 16). Mary, Christ's mother, was a pure virgin set apart by God as a holy vessel. Bathsheba was a married woman whose husband was one of David's mighty men, yet she fell into adultery with David. Ruth was a Moabite, a widow and a minority under the curse of the Law, yet her faith delivered her from her past, and she broke generational curses. Tamar was a bitter woman who posed as a prostitute to retaliate against Judah, becoming pregnant to embarrass him, and Rahab was a prostitute who turned her life and destiny around. Women are not normally mentioned in the Jewish male-dominated genealogy. However, the names of Bathsheba, Rahab, and Tamar are there, not to remind us of their pasts or failures, but to demonstrate the power of redemption and forgiveness.

The spiritual principle as to why God blessed Rahab and her future generations is she was the firstfruits or the first person converted to the Hebrew God to enter the Promised Land. Just as Ruth was a firstfruits woman of God from Moab, and broke the curse of the Moabites, the firstfruits blessing means that when the first is given to God then the remaining parts receive a special blessing.

Firstfruits Mothers

Today in the body of Christ ministers present the theme of firstfruits related to tithes, offerings, and financial increase. However, the greatest firstfruits blessing is when a person becomes the first believer in a family of unbelievers. I have friends in ministry in which the wife says she is from four generations of believers and her husband is from four generations of heathens!

I am blessed to be from four generations of Christians—three generations of ministers with myself being the fourth generation. I receive letters from men and women who remind me how fortunate and blessed I am to have such a legacy and heritage of ministry in my background. One man from prison wrote and told me that if he had strong men of God in his background and a father such as I had, he believes he would have taken a different path and would have never ended up making bad decisions that led him to a life in prison.

If you are the first in your family to enter into a covenant with Christ, you are the firstfruits and can lay claim to the firstfruits blessing, planting the seed for your unborn children or grand-children to come under the umbrella of covenant favor and the covenant of redemption. If you have enjoyed generations of believers in your family, then you are enjoying the harvest of a firstfruits blessing, initiated by the first generation of believers in your bloodline where the seeds of increase were planted and the fruits of blessing are hanging on your tree.

CHAPTER 5

The POWER of a MOTHER'S PROPHECY

IT WAS THE YEAR 1918, THE DAYS BEFORE GOOD MEDICINE and skilled doctors. Certain sicknesses could take the life of children, and the mortality rate was high. An outstanding Christian woman with strong faith was called upon by neighbors to pray for their sick child. While crossing a fence, the woman vowed to God that if He would heal this child and in the future give her a son, she would dedicate him for ministry. God healed the child that night, and the woman who prayed became pregnant. When her son was born, she dedicated him to ministry.

The mother wanted to give the boy a *prophetic name*, so she picked one with the meaning, "to speak out loud." However, when he began to speak, the family learned the lad had a terrible stuttering problem. He was mocked in school, and at times would run away from school in embarrassment. The mockery was so bad that at age fifteen he ran away from home.

After his parents and others prayed for him, he returned home at age seventeen and began playing basketball. During one game he collapsed to the ground and was sent home, diagnosed with tuberculosis. As he became weak, losing weight and unable to eat or stand up, his mother kept reminding him that God was going to raise him up, heal his stuttering, and he would reach multitudes as a preacher of the gospel.

After one hundred sixty days in bed, the family heard of a tent evangelist having great results in praying for the sick. They made arrangements to transport the sick teenager on a mattress in the back of a vehicle. His sister told him, "God is going to heal you!" That night, under the tent, the minister prayed, commanding the devil to get his hands off the young man. Suddenly the lad jumped up from the mattress and began to testify without stuttering—and never stuttered again. From that moment he followed the Lord and became a minister of the gospel, just as his mother had predicted.

He purchased a tent and drew some of the largest crowds of his generation, seeing amazing miracles of healing. He built a major Christian university and lived seventy-four years beyond the time of his healing, passing at age ninety-one. His name was Oral Roberts. He was healed because his mother held on and refused to give up on her vow to God.[1]

When Is a Prayer a Prophecy?

The power to alter circumstances is released in the prophetic prayers of mothers and fathers. Modern scholars interpret the meaning of prophesying as proclaiming the gospel. However, proclaiming the gospel is preaching and teaching (Matt. 28:19–20; Mark 16:15). The word *preach* is found in more than forty verses in the New Testament. The common Greek word is *kerysso*, meaning, "to proclaim or to herald a message." The root word was used for a person who was sent by a king into a city with a proclamation he read in public. The word *teach* in Greek is *didasko*, and means, "to learn from instruction." People often confuse the word prophesy with prophecy. The word *prophecy* is used in most contexts with the biblical messages predicting future events. The word *prophesy,* is *propheteuo*, and means, "to foretell events under divine inspiration; to exercise the office of a prophet." Biblically, when thinking of prophetic voices we often read of men operating in this gift. However, the Bible identifies several women as prophetesses—a female operating in this inspirational gift (Exod. 15:20; Judg. 4:4; 2 Chron. 34:22).

Luke records where two pregnant women, both cousins, were also inspired by the Holy Spirit with divine utterances so significant that their prophetic insights are recorded in the New Testament. Elizabeth was the elder, and Mary the younger—both pregnant and both informed by the angel Gabriel they would birth sons. The names of both sons were known before their births—John, Elizabeth's son, and Jesus, the son of Mary. Elizabeth spoke a great blessing upon Mary, which is still spoken by those in the Catholic tradition:

> Then she spoke out with a loud voice and said, "Blessed are you among women, and blessed is the fruit of your womb!"
> —LUKE 1:42

Mary replied to Elizabeth's good news, and her words are also recalled by devout religious seekers around the world:

> For He has regarded the lowly state of His maidservant;
> For behold, henceforth all generations will call me blessed.
> —LUKE 1:48

In the New Testament era, Mary was a common name among Israeli women, appearing sixty-one times in fifty-three different verses in the Bible. The oldest sister of Moses and Aaron was called Miriam (Exod. 15:20), which is the English form of Mary. There is Mary the mother of Christ (Matt. 1:16); Mary Magdalene (Matt. 27:56); Mary the mother of James and John (Matt. 27:56); Mary from Bethany (Luke 10:42); and Mary the mother of Cleophas (John 19:25). Mary is called the wife of Joseph and when speaking of Christ she is called "His mother" eight times in Matthew (Matt. 1:18; 2:11, 13–14, 20–21; 12:46; 13:55).

Christ's Father was *heavenly*, but His mother was *earthly*. Imagine Christ explaining the difference between His Father's and mother's sides of the family. When asked how old He was He could say, "I'm older than My mother but the same age of My Father." To the question, "Where were You born?" He could reply, "On My mother's side in Bethlehem, but on My Father's side I have always existed." When asked where He lived, He could explain, "On My mother's side I've lived in Nazareth, but on My Father's side I'm just visiting Earth for a few years." When asked what He owned, the answer could be, "On My mother's side I borrow everything, but on My Father's side We own everything you see." When He revealed He was going to die, He could give these details: "On My mother's side I will die in Jerusalem, but on My Father's side I will live on forever." As Jesus, people viewed Him as an earthly man, but as Christ He was the anointed Son of God.

Christ's first miracle was motivated by His mother's instructions. In the ancient days a wedding celebration continued for seven days (Judg. 14:15–18). The greatest concern during a week of celebration and feasting would be to run out of food and drink. In John 2 they had run out of drink, which was concerning to Mary. When Mary approached Christ for help, He, as the saying goes, "blew her off" and said, "My hour [to perform miracles] has not yet come." Without responding to Him, Mary turned to the servants and said, "Whatever He says to you, do it" (John 2:4–5).

At that moment Mary gave the *mission statement* for Christ's entire ministry. Whatever He or God tells you to do, just do it. Blessing is only released through obedience, and miracles are manifested when we do what He says! Christ was moved by the faith of His mother, and the first biblical miracle was turning water into wine at the wedding feast. There is a certain authority that is released when a mother turns her attention to Christ and begins to speak a word that will alter the present situation and create a miracle for the future.

Standing Between Life and Death

This story begins with a West Virginia preacher's son, a football player and drummer who, by tenth grade, was consumed with drinking hard liquor. His addiction was so severe that he could drink Jack Daniel's whiskey straight without a chaser. The bondage became so bad that there was not a day when he did not have alcohol in his body—day and night. One fateful night he decided to drink more than he ever had and be the *life of the party*. Since his father was going to preach out of town, this meant his weekend would be free from any parental supervision, so he set up a party at the house of a friend whose parents were also out of town for the weekend. That night it started with a few drinks, but in no time he was completely intoxicated.

When his friends saw how *wasted* he was they decided to borrow a car and take him to someone's home who would take care of him, without his parents knowing what had occurred. As the alcohol hit his stomach, he immediately vomited it back up. He had drunk on an empty stomach, mixed dark and clear liquors, and smoked pot on top of all this. He was a physical wreck and in serious condition. He had no idea that at the same time he was vomiting and delirious, God was speaking to his father, who was two hours into driving to another town to minister. His dad heard God say, "Turn your car around. Your son is in trouble." His dad immediately turned around and began heading back home to Nitro, West Virginia.

Back in Nitro, in the car with "friends," the fellow began blacking out because his head was spinning, and he began violently vomiting, as only hard-core alcoholic drink was in his stomach. The alcohol was doing its damage, as blood was now mixing with the vomit. He would later learn that he had a rupture between his stomach and his esophagus. His friends became so scared they dropped him off behind a house in an alleyway. There he was lying in his blood, out of his mind, with no help and no way of getting help. The miracle was that his father, not knowing where he was, was led by the Holy Spirit and found him lying on the side of the road. His father immediately loaded him into the car, and the boy began crying, because he knew he was dying and was in a lost condition.

After checking with a doctor who said there was nothing they could do, they instructed the father not to let him go to sleep. His mother and dad took him home and put him in the hands of God. He recalls going in and out of consciousness while his *mother* was praying over him.

He wrote:

> At one point I remember the voices of demons speaking over me that I would not make it through the night. Immediately when I heard these voices, my mom would respond with a rebuke that answered the lies I heard from those voices. I heard in my head, "You will die tonight," and Mom would

yell out, "Devil, you are a liar; my son will not die tonight." I remember her saying, "We prophesied over you while you were in my belly that you would preach the gospel to the nations of the world. You will not die until you fulfill the assignment God has placed upon your life." All night my parents prayed for me, keeping me awake as much as they could, finally allowing me to sleep around five in the morning. Five hours earlier I had breathed in a Breathalyzer while in an almost comatose state. I remember waking up at 7:30 in the morning, feeling as though I had slept all night. I didn't have a headache, no hangover, and the hole in my esophagus had closed. The bleeding had completely stopped, and God had completely healed me. That was my first personal encounter with the saving and delivering power of Jesus Christ. He had healed me and given me a second chance. Since that moment I have never touched another drink of alcohol, or smoked another joint. I was free and free indeed!

Today this young man, Mark Casto, is married with three children and pastors the OCI ministries in Cleveland, Tennessee.[2] He credits his mother and father's all-night intercession for both his healing and his deliverance. His mother understood the power of a mother prophesying the promises of God over her prodigal son.

Praying Them Back Home

Growing up, one of my special ministry mentors was Dr. E. L. Terry. He was very bold, at times brazen, and always interesting to hear. His true stories became legendary among the younger ministers, including myself, Jentezen Franklin, and Marcus Lamb, all who admired his reckless and unwavering faith. One of his most remarkable stories involved a young man who had run away from home and how his mother prayed for his return.

Many years ago Dr. Terry was preaching a revival in North Carolina. One night during the altar service, a woman approached him and asked if he would pray that her son would come back home, and that it would happen before the sun rose in the morning. Without asking for details, E. L. went into a powerful prayer of agreement, commanding that the boy would come home before the sun came up in the morning. After he prayed a fervent prayer, the mother began rejoicing and thanking God out loud, "Thank You, Lord, he's coming home tonight!"

The pastor heard the woman shouting as she began walking around the sanctuary saying, "He's coming home; thank You, Lord." The pastor asked E. L., "What did you say to her?"

He replied, "I agreed with her that her son would come home before the sun rose!"

The pastor replied, "Oh my, you didn't?" He then explained that the son had run away from home more than three years ago, and the mother had never heard from him and wasn't sure if he was dead or alive. But she always believed he was still out there somewhere.

The woman was determined to stay at the church, praying and thanking God all night. The pastor, E. L., and the pastor's wife decided they may as well remain with her at the church. By the early morning the mother was fully alert, as the others were scattered across the congregation kneeling half-asleep. The mother, during more than five hours, never ceased to thank God and prophesy, "He's coming home...thank God, he's coming back." The pastor was concerned how she would respond when the sun rose and her son was not back with her.

At about 3:30 a.m., someone was heard banging on the front

door of the church. The mother ran to the doors, and the pastor arose thinking it was the police wondering why the church lights were on so late and what was going on. Instead, when she opened the door, a young man fell into her arms yelling, "Mama, Mama!" To the delight of the mother and the shock of the other three, there she stood hugging her prodigal son.

They discovered the boy was hundreds of miles away, when suddenly he had an unquenchable urge to go home and see his mother again. He could not get a bus ticket so he began hitchhiking. Eventually a man wearing a cowboy hat and driving a Cadillac stopped and asked him where he was headed. He told the man, and the fellow replied, "I'm not headed in that direction."

The boy broke down and said, "I must get home. I ran away three years ago, and I want to go home and see my mama."

The man's heart was touched. Smiling he replied, "Get in, son, we are headed home!"

One amazing fact is that when the boy had run away, his mother's church was in a different building in a different part of town. As they entered the town, the mother's church was now on a main street. The boy saw the signs and the lights on, and said, "Stop here! That's my mother's church."

The man replied, "Son, no one is going be in church at three thirty in the morning." But he did stop, and the young man could hear his mother's voice through the doors. The rest is history.[3]

Praying for Addicted Sons and Daughters

One fact must remain clear when a dad, a mother, or both parents begin praying for the redemption and deliverance of a child or loved one: never allow the visible circumstances to change the focus of your prayer. There are times when things will appear to *get worse* before there is a *breakthrough*, as battles always precede breakthroughs.

In the early days of my grandfather John Bava's generation, alcohol was outlawed, prostitution was illegal, and there were no youths smoking marijuana. Fast-forward to today. The federal and state governments began legalizing bondages to collect a *sin tax*, bringing more cash into their tax-and-spend coffers. We have transitioned from hard-core moonshine to more than three hundred types of beers, wines, and alcoholic beverages. Now states are legalizing the use of marijuana, a drug that not only affects the pancreas, liver, and lungs, but is also a gateway drug to harder drugs. America is a society of addicted individuals—addicted to alcohol, to illegal and prescription drugs, to pornography, and to gambling. Energy drinks are popular, indicating people are desiring a pick-me-up or a good feeling that somehow they are not getting in their daily routine of life. For a parent, seeing an addicted child who refuses help, counseling, or rehab is troubling and frightening. Some mom's or dad's son or daughter dies every day from an overdose or in a drunken collision. However, there is a method to pray for the loved one who is addicted.

Years ago a young man who was raised by a godly praying mother began rebelling against her authority, turning to wrong friends, alcohol and drugs, living the life of a full-blown addict. His craving for alcohol was so intense that he drank beer for breakfast and smoked marijuana continually. Slowly, one by one, his friends began dying. One was shot by another while getting into a fight over the last bottle of whiskey. The shooter, in his early twenties, was afterward arrested for burglary, and because of the shooting was sentenced to twenty years in prison. Another friend died in a fight after breaking his neck, and another died at age thirty-six from cirrhosis of the liver. Still another man who partied with him went to sleep one night, and a seventeen-year-old girl with whom he had been partying and arguing came into his room and shot him to death in the head. Three other men who were rough beer drinkers and drug peddlers all died—one from a drug overdose, one was killed in Atlanta after buying drugs, and the third fell drunken into the street and was run over by a car. Still others died from dirty needles, stabbings, and accidents. The difference between this man and the others is that he had a *mother* who never stopped praying for his protection and his salvation.

The young man who survived many dangerous and near-death encounters recalls his mother praying for him so loudly that even when he was outside he could hear her voice. She never gave up and was determined that her son would be delivered and serve the Lord. The circumstances never got better, only worse. He was arrested for drug possession, carrying a concealed weapon, and assaulting a police officer. During this entire time, he confessed that the Holy Spirit continually convicted him, even when he appeared to be ignoring his mother's warnings.

Finally, time and conviction clashed, opening his understanding and turning his heart from darkness to light. He became sick and tired of being spiritually blind and bound. Today this man, Terry Lamunyon, who is a Christian biker, works for our ministry at VOE and OCI, taking care of the grounds and the facilities. His love for the Lord radiates from him, and his commitment to ministry is unwavering.[4] The chains were broken because a Christian mother had birthed a son whom she refused to give up or give in to the enemy, and she bombarded heaven to break the veil of bondage on her son.

In these amazing miracle deliverance and healing stories of Oral Roberts, Mark Casto, Terry Lamunyon, and the young man from North Carolina, a woman, a mother of faith, used the power of prayer and confessed the promises of God to strike hard on the spirit of death and destruction.

Learn to Speak
Life and Not Death

It seems that people are attracted toward the negative. Negative news always has better ratings than good news. In fact, media outlets note that good news stories actually bore most viewers. When there is a breaking news alert people tune in better. When there is a story involving Israel, the viewership increases, as many Christians and Jews are interested in events emerging out of Israel and the Middle East. There is a reason that most twenty-four-hour cable and satellite news coverage groups place two opposing views behind a table, letting them fight it out. This stirs the emotions of a viewer who chooses one side over the other, like two football teams or two boxers. Even some self-appointed watchdog ministers have understood how controversy pulls in viewers, and they freely call names exposing heretics, which causes a stir, pulling in curious viewers who thirst to hear an exposé on the next heretic of the faith. Sad to say, harsh, negative words bring the termites and roaches out of the woodwork.

Being continually bombarded by pessimism, unbelief, and negative comments, it is easy for some believers who are praying for what seems to be impossible to become faithless and make comments that tear apart the foundation of what we are building. Solomon wrote that, "Death and life are in the power of the tongue" (Prov. 18:21). This Hebrew word *power* is not the normal word, but is the Hebrew word *yad*, meaning, "a hand." When a rabbi in a synagogue reads a Torah scroll, he uses an ornament called a *yad*, a long silver pointer with a small hand on top, with the index finger extended, which prevents the reader from touching the Torah scroll with his hands. The word *hand*, found 1,312 times in the English translation of the Bible, is usually the Hebrew word *yad*. Thus the human *tongue* can become the hand that can hold on to life or bring forth death.

The power of the spoken word is obvious when reading the Creation account in Genesis 1. Everything came out of nothing, as the *invisible forces* holding the universe in place are atoms, made up of protons and neutrons surrounded by electrons, all which can respond and be altered by the Word of God. Gravity was reversed when Christ walked upon water, and it will again lose its hold when the dead are raised and the living saints are changed, caught up to meet the Lord in the clouds (1 Thess. 4:16–17). God's formula to create something from nothing is as follows: "God said…" (Gen. 1:3), followed by, "God made…" (Gen. 1:7), then "God saw…" (Gen. 1:10). When praying in faith for what we have not seen, we must *say it first*, then *make it* by continually hanging on and not giving up, and eventually we will *see it* come to pass. During the six days of Creation, when the work was completed God said, "It was good" (Gen. 1:4, 10, 12, 18, 21, 25). Every good gift God has planned for you comes from above (James 1:17). You must expect a good outcome, but you must also maintain a verbal agreement while anticipating the results to your prayers, moving from saying to seeing.

The spirit world—from both realms—observes the confessions we make. When entering a redemptive covenant, *believing* is only one part of the process, as with the heart you believe but with the mouth *confession* is made unto salvation (Rom. 10:10). The Greek word *confession* is *homologeo*, which means, "to say the same thing." It refers to coming into complete agreement with something or someone. In the Hebrew the word *confess* is found in Psalms 32:5, being the Hebrew word *yada*, which is translated in the English Bible as the word *knew* (Gen. 4:1), and *acknowledge* (Prov. 3:6). It requires accurate knowledge—knowing the truth—to make a confession, lining up with the promises you are claiming.

Both God and Satan observe the conversations of the righteous. When Job lost his family and all his wealth, he never blamed God, as we read, "In all this Job did not sin nor charge God with wrong" (Job 1:22). Satan expected Job to sin with his mouth, curse God, and throw away his faith (v. 11). However, God knew Job's heart and believed he would maintain his integrity, which he did (Job 2:3). This clash between "he will curse," and "he won't curse" reveals the clash between God's confidence in your integrity and Satan doubting your determination to stand without flinching. If we stand in intercession for a family member, interceding for a redemptive covenant, we must believe what we pray and hold on to our prayer, as by this we "hold fast the confession of our hope without wavering" (Heb. 10:23; see also James 1:6). Wavering is to speak faith one day and unbelief the next, believe the possibility one day and deny the possibility the following day. If we pray in faith and speak in doubt, the adversary, who understands the laws of answered prayer, knows he has gained the upper hand in hindering our answer.

To prevent weariness in prayer, one must move from flowing words to aggressive declarations and confessions. I once saw a mother move from prayer to prophetic declarations. She was in aggressive intercession in her house, praying for a wayward son who was under a direct assault of the enemy. For about fifteen minutes her petition for God's help and delivering power filled the room, echoing through the entire house. Suddenly the prayer shifted, and she began pronouncing declarations addressed to the spiritual powers assaulting her bloodline. She lifted her voice and declared: *"Satan, you have no right in my house. This house belongs to the Lord! My son belongs to God and not to you. In Jesus's name I break your stronghold over his mind and his life, and I take authority over the darkness in the name of Jesus Christ."* The words of her prayer could be felt. But when she shifted into the power of the declaration, divine energy pierced every area of spiritual darkness in the room. That night there was a breakthrough for the son, as he confessed and emptied three garbage bags of junk from his room.

There are three ways to make a prophetic declaration—meaning a spiritual proclamation announcing your expectations for the future and your confidence in God's promises. The first way is by discovering specific promises in the Word and coming into agreement with them verbally, praying them each day during your devotional time. The second comes when praying more intensely, mixing biblical promises with the prophetic declarations, joining the two together as you pray, making a verbal confession with God and the Holy Spirit. The third is a more aggressive method. Your spirit becomes agitated to the point of birthing a fiery zeal that burns within your spirit. As you pray, you become angry at the darts, arrows, and traps the enemy is using against your family or your children, and you refuse to just passively lie down and take it. Your prayers of agreement with the covenant Word become reinforced with rebukes against the powers of darkness. Remember, Jesus rebuked sickness and demons in people (Matt. 17:18; Mark 9:25), but He also rebuked violent storms in the atmosphere (Matt. 8:26). The New Testament Greek word used for *rebuke* is stronger than just telling someone off. It means to censure or forbid, meaning that when Christ rebuked demons He forbade them from speaking and forbade them from coming back into their victim (Mark 9:25). Your rebuke addressed to the powers of darkness is a command, not a request, forbidding them from further advancement against their targets.

There is a great significance in the woman resisting Satan. When the serpent tempted Eve, God set a hatred (enmity) between women and Satan's influence. We read:

> And I will put enmity between you and the woman, and between your offspring and her Offspring; He will bruise and tread your head underfoot, and you will lie in wait and bruise His heel.
> —GENESIS 3:15, AMP

God said nothing to Adam about having hostility. Men tend to be more earthly, and women more spiritual. After all, Eve gave in to the serpent's temptation because she was hungry for knowledge, to be wiser, to become more like God, and her desire pulled her into eating from the tree of knowledge (Gen. 3:1–6). Adam's earthliness is seen in the fact that he consisted of the three main elements of the planet: *earth* (he was made from dust), *wind* (God breathed breath into him), and *water* (the garden was watered by a mist from the ground [Gen. 2:6–7]). Woman came from out of man and not out of the dust. Adam and Eve would deal with two seeds: the earthly seed of agriculture from the ground of earth, and the seed of man, which would produce a living offspring with an eternal soul and spirit. Man would till the soil to make the seeds of plants and trees produce fruit, but the woman would carry the seed of a man, and birth a living soul. Adam must protect the earthly seed from thorns and weeds, but the woman must defend the seed she births from the power of the serpent. It requires enmity, or hostility, to fight the serpent and his dark powers.

Before the encounter with the serpent in the garden, Adam's companion is called *woman*. After the Fall Adam calls her *Eve*, the Hebrew name meaning, "mother of life," or the mother of all living beings. It can be pointed out that the woman who introduced death to humanity through sin would birth in her womb the future "seed" that would bring life to all humanity; thus her seed would bruise the head of the serpent.

Fathers are often consumed with earthly cares and worldly activities. However, a woman of God despises evil and hates the serpent, who is Satan. Within each godly woman and mother is a God-given gift to persist in prayer and hold on until victory occurs. The woman in Luke 18 persisted to approach the judge, without wavering, until she got his attention and he moved on her behalf. God spoke the first prophecy in the Bible in Genesis 3:15 to the woman. Spiritual authority is released to the daughters and handmaidens of the Most High, giving them spiritual authority to prophesy to their seed. To prophesy is to speak into the future what you believe for and expect it to occur, versus what is happening at the moment and what the enemy is setting up for evil. Transfer the scriptures from your mind to your mouth, from your thoughts to your words. Then speak to your mountain (Matt. 17:20).

Speaking As Though It Were

Paul alluded to Abraham when he wrote:

> (As it is written, "I have made you a father of many nations") in the presence of Him whom he believed—God, who gives life to the dead and calls those things which do not exist as though they did.
>
> —ROMANS 4:17

When Abraham's reproduction possibilities were gone and Sarah's womb was dead, God was calling him a "father of many nations" (Gen. 17:5). Years before Isaac was born, God said He had (already, present tense) made him a father of many nations (v. 5): "I have made you a father of many nations." From the first promise of fatherhood (Gen. 12:2–3), until the moment he held his infant son

(Gen. 21:1–3), was twenty-five years. Yet, God released encouraging words to energize Abraham's faith—"I have made you a father." This is because God speaks things before they happen as though they have already happened!

God puts His plans, purposes, and will in your spirit before you ever see His plan and purpose fulfilled. Unbelief is released when we *question* why we are not seeing the promises come to pass. Humans react upon what they see, hear, and feel. God, however, begins with nothing to create something. When we do not see results, it does not mean God is not moving quietly behind the scenes. This is where faith and patience undergird the mind and spirit as we wait for the promise to come to pass, as it is written: "That you do not become sluggish, but imitate those who through faith and patience inherit the promises" (Heb. 6:12).

As believers we have a choice of living in one of two realms: faith or unbelief, anxiety or patience, and the *did* and the *do*. The *did* group can recall the great works of God in the past, but are fearful of their futures, not knowing what they will *do* if things don't work out or if God doesn't *come through*. As we become older, we live in the *did* realm, relating stories of what God *did* in the past for us. Testimonies reveal what God *has done* for us, but confessing the Word is identifying what God *will do* for us. What God "did" should make us "do," or act upon our faith for the future, as "faith without works [corresponding action] is dead" (James 2:26). I once heard a young minister, Craig Mosgrove, say, "When your memories get bigger than your vision, you will die out to your future." This is why the Bible teaches that without a vision people will perish (Prov. 29:18).

We must recall God's provision and blessings of the past, not dwelling in the memory, but using the memory to encourage our spirits for the future blessings that we are praying for, including the salvation of our family. God calls things that are not as though they already were. We could say He is "prophesying the future." Once we have a Word of assurance about our situations, we can lay hold of the promise and begin to speak in the future tense of what God will do, and not just recall a memory of what God did.

CHAPTER 6

FROM THE WOMB OF MERCY

MANY OF THE EARLY FOUNDING FATHERS OF AMERICA were raised in the home with a Christian mother and with a Bible. It was George Washington who said, "All I am I owe to my mother. I attribute all my success in life to the moral, intellectual, and physical education I received from her."[1]

When God created woman, she was named Eve. Her name in Hebrew is *Chavvah*, whose root in Hebrew means, "a life giver." Eve is called the "mother of all living" (Gen. 3:20). Note that when Adam awoke from his sleep, he saw her, calling her "woman" (Gen. 2:23), the Hebrew word being *ishshah*. Before the Fall in the garden, the name "woman" is used to describe the wife of Adam (Gen. 2:22–23; 3:1, 2, 4, 6, 12–13, 15–16). Only after the Fall did Adam call her Eve (Gen. 3:20).

> And the LORD God caused a deep sleep to fall on Adam, and he slept; and He took one of his ribs, and closed up the flesh in its place. Then the rib which the LORD

God had taken from man He made into a woman, and He brought her to the man.

—GENESIS 2:21–22

The word *rib* here, *tsela*, is the same Hebrew word used in 1 Kings 7:3 for the *beams* in Solomon's temple. It can also be used as a board or the arch in a doorway. The same word is used in Exodus 25:14, referring to the *sides* of the ark of the covenant where the poles were placed (Exod. 27:7). When we read that God placed Adam in a deep sleep, taking a rib from him to create Eve, the meaning can also be that God took a "side" from him and formed a woman from a side of Adam.

This understanding brings to light a commonly held view that when it comes to a man marrying a woman, opposites attract. Literally every couple I know is opposite—not in their beliefs but in their likes and dislikes. Often if the husband is humorous, the wife is more serious. If he is impatient, she exercises more patience. If he is emotional, she tends to operate more rationally. It is the nature of a man to follow his wife and to leave his parents, cleaving to her for support. Metaphorically, just as a beam in a house supports the structure, the wife and mother become the "pillar" (beam) of the family.

Every man, with the exception of the first man, Adam, must enter the world through the *womb* of a woman. The womb of a woman is the development and birth chamber of all infants, male and female. The first reference to the woman's *womb* was when God informed Rebekah that "Two nations are in your womb, two peoples shall be separated from your body" (Gen. 25:23). The Hebrew word for *womb* here is *beten*, the root word means a hollow, or the bosom or body of anything. In another scripture God opened Leah's womb, and she gave birth to Reuben (Gen. 29:31). The Hebrew word translated as *womb* here is *rechem*. This word is also found in Genesis 30:22, Exodus 13:2, Numbers 8:16, and other places.

Words in Hebrew start out with a root usually of three consonants. Then the prefixes and suffixes are added to form the complete word and provide numerous meanings from the one root. Many root letters can actually have several different meanings. *Rechem* consists of three Hebrew letters: *resh*, *chet*, and a closed *mem* (root, RCM). The letter *resh* can represent a head and can allude to a person. The *chet* can represent a fence, with the closed *mem* being something hidden, but when the letter is opened it can allude to water. Thus the symbolic image of the Hebrew word *rechem*, for *womb*, is a child in water who is hidden and protected within the womb of its mother!

In the Old Testament one of the Hebrew words for *mercy* is *racham*, translated in the English translation as *compassion, mercy*, and *pity* (Exod. 33:19; Isa. 27:11, 30:18; Hosea 14:3; Zech. 1:12). This word has the same three root Hebrew letters (RCM). In the Hebrew the word *racham* is used forty-three times in the Old Testament with six references in the Book of Hosea (Hosea 1:6–7; 2:1, 4, 23; 14:3). The narrative in Hosea reveals the love the prophet has for his wife, Gomer, a prostitute. Hosea expresses his love, compassion, and mercy toward his straying companion, as God compares her unfaithfulness to Israel's backslidings.[2] The word connection between the *womb* of a woman with the word for *mercy* and *compassion* is significant. This word seeks to bring security to the life of the one to whom the compassion is being felt.[3]

The Hebrew word *rechem* is used for the first nine months that a child is in its mother's belly, as the water surrounding the fetus protects the infant from outer dangers. The womb was designed by the Almighty to be a place of *mercy and protection* for the mother's child. If a woman has natural affection, she will enjoy a God-given attachment between her and the infant she carries long before the child's physical birth. This motherly connection is evident in our culture, considering the numbers of *men* who walk out on their newborn infants, having nothing to do with them, leaving the mother alone to raise the child. A father may have provided the *seed* in a few seconds, but the mother provided the *womb* for nine months. We read, "Can a woman forget her nursing child, and not have compassion on the son of her womb" (Isa. 49:15). A mother with normal affections can never forget her child.

Many women also are imparted with a natural caregiver instinct, becoming a wife who cares for her husband, a mother caring for her children, and a caregiver as she becomes older helping those who are unable to help themselves. The link between the womb and compassion indicates that a woman's love, compassion, and mercy are not just a thought in her mind, but begin within her belly, the location of her inner spirit (Prov. 20:27). Her love, pain, joy, and happiness are all internal emotions that her life revolves around. Imagine how God used the womb of a woman to bring the Messiah into the world! The most compassionate and merciful human to ever be born in the womb of a woman was Christ; the womb of Mary being the belly of compassion and mercy.

Throughout the four Gospels, Mary His mother appears from the story of the Immaculate Conception to John standing with her at the Crucifixion. One debated question has been, "Whatever happened to Joseph, the husband of Mary?" Why is Joseph absent during Christ's ministry?

Whatever Happened to Joseph?

Joseph was not the biological father of Christ, as Christ was conceived through the Holy Spirit (Matt. 1:18). In that day the moment a man was engaged to marry a woman, they were considered married by the community, although the actual act of consummation and the wedding celebration occurred months after the initial engagement, when the man would receive his bride and take her to his father's house for the bridal supper and celebration. Joseph was espoused (engaged) to Mary, and when he heard she was pregnant, he began preparing a bill of divorcement, when the angel of the Lord informed Joseph that Mary was with child from the Holy Spirit (Matt. 1:17–20).

In the biblical record Joseph was from the house of David (Luke 1:27) but was living in Galilee, in Nazareth (Luke 2:4). Two genealogies list the name of Joseph; one as the *husband of Mary* (Matt. 1:1–17) and Christ being "supposed" the son of Joseph (Luke 3:23). Mary was espoused (engaged) to Joseph (Matt. 1:18), when an angel visited him instructing him to take Mary (Matt. 1:20–21). Joseph was present when the shepherds arrived at the stable to worship the infant king, and months later when the wise men arrived bringing gifts (Luke 2:8–16; Matt. 2:1–11).

Joseph is to be commended for obeying the Holy Spirit, including fleeing with Mary and the child to Egypt and returning to Nazareth under angelic instruction (Matt. 2:11–21). We know that Joseph's occupation was a carpenter, which in that day could also be a stone mason, not just a woodworking specialist. The final biblical narrative that mentions Joseph is when he and Mary attended a feast in Jerusalem, and the community caravan departed not knowing that the young Jesus, age twelve, was missing from the group. He was later found at the temple in Jerusalem, going about His (heavenly) Father's business (Luke 2:42–52).

There is no biblical record indicating what happened to Joseph, as by the time Christ began His public ministry at age thirty (Luke 3:23), Joseph is not mentioned as part of the ministry team. He is not present at the Crucifixion, the Resurrection, or listed in the meeting prior to the Day of Pentecost (Acts 1:13–17). There have been many questions as to what happened to Joseph, the husband of Mary.

There are non-inspired writings that attempt to give details of Joseph's early history and his death. For the sake of our study, here is an example. In one account Joseph passed when he was one hundred eleven years of age in the twenty-sixth month of Abib. The story alleges that Christ Himself related the details of Joseph's life while sitting with His disciples on the Mount of Olives. According to this tradition Joseph was from Bethlehem, the tribe of Judah, a carpenter by trade and was made a priest in the temple. He was married, and his wife gave birth to four sons and two daughters. Joseph's wife eventually died, and he left the temple and went with his sons to practice the art of carpentry.

This story alleged that Mary lived at the temple from three years of age, serving there until twelve. The priest began searching out a righteous man to marry her. Twelve names of men from Judah were selected, with Joseph being chosen by lots. Mary lived with a family until she was fourteen, at which time she conceived from the Holy Spirit, giving birth to Christ at age fifteen. Joseph was willing to put her away when the angel Gabriel told him to take her for his wife. In the narrative Christ is said to have told His disciples that He was born in a cave near the tomb of Rachel in Bethlehem.

Joseph, being much older than Mary, eventually became advanced in age, when an angel of the Lord informed him that he would die. He traveled to the temple to pray, returning to Nazareth where he died of a disease. He is said to have lived forty years unmarried. The story continues that on his deathbed in Nazareth, Joseph was wretched and fearful of death. Thus Jesus was said to have begun intercession for him to prevent demons from snatching

Joseph's soul. God sent Michael and Gabriel to wrap the soul of Joseph and carry it away.[4]

This story is believed and accepted by some in the traditional Roman Church. However, there are numerous difficulties with the content. The first is the explanation that Joseph was previously married and gave birth to six other children before taking Mary for his wife. This theory would explain why some suggest that the "brothers and sisters" of Christ listed in Matthew 13 were not from Mary but a previous wife of Joseph, thus keeping with the Roman Church tradition that Mary never conceived other children or was forever virgin. However, notice that four brothers and sisters are all living in Nazareth.

We do know from the New Testament that Mary and Joseph had other children after the birth of Christ.

> When He had come to His own country, He taught them in their synagogue, so that they were astonished and said, "Where did this Man get this wisdom and these mighty works? Is this not the carpenter's son? Is not His mother called Mary? And His brothers James, Joses, Simon, and Judas? And His sisters, are they not all with us? Where then did this Man get all these things?" So they were offended at Him.
> —MATTHEW 13:54–57

The explanation of Joseph being a priest at the temple does not fit with the Law of Moses. The Levites from the tribe of Levi were set aside as the priests, and not those from Judah, the tribe of Joseph. These stories were embellished based upon traditions and not any known biblical facts.

The often pondered question is: "Why does Joseph not appear in any narrative from the beginning of Christ's ministry to the Ascension?" The clear answer is that at some point Joseph died, between the periods when Christ was twelve and the time He was baptized. These seventeen years in the life of Christ are called the *missing years*, and from a biblical narrative these seventeen years are *silent years* where it appears that Christ remained in Nazareth, either working with Joseph or remaining with His mother and somehow providing for her. It appears that Mary followed Christ at times during His ministry.

It would be speculative to come up with numerous reasons why God allowed Joseph to die. In the beginning of Christ's life, there was clear danger to the child during Herod's rule. Joseph led Mary and the infant Christ child to Egypt for an unknown period of time. They returned with the intent of living in Bethlehem, but they were informed by the angel of the Lord to dwell in Galilee in Nazareth.

It is significant, however, that Mary His mother remained close to Christ. There were many things she kept hidden in her heart (Luke 2:19, 51). The death of Joseph would make Mary a widow, which in that day was not an easy position to be in. Christ paid careful attention to widows. During His first sermon in Nazareth, Christ related the story of a Gentile widow at Zarephath who fed Elijah during a forty-two month famine (Luke 4:24–26). At the temple in Jerusalem there were boxes shaped like trumpets in which people would cast their coins. Christ saw a widow woman casting two copper coins, all that she had. Christ commented that she had given more than the others combined (Mark 12:42–44). Christ raised the dead and only son of a widow woman from Nain, after having compassion on her (Luke 7:12–15). One of Christ's parables dealt with a widow woman needing justice, who was persistent in her determination to receive judicial justice (Luke 18:1–8). This emphasis on widows may have been motivated by Christ's compassion, knowing His own mother, Mary, was in this same position.

If Joseph passed away during those seventeen years, Mary was not just a widow without a husband, but she was also a single mother. It appears that Christ stayed at Nazareth until about age thirty when He began His public ministry. For a single mother who today is raising a family, the idea of Christ being raised and living with His mother—without an earthly father—should encourage you that He is moved with compassion toward both widows and any woman with children where a father is absent or deceased.

Being Born Again

The womb giving natural birth is a picture of the new birth. The apostle John records a late-night conversation with a prominent man in Jerusalem named Nicodemus. Even the Jewish Encyclopedia recognized this man when it reads:

> Nicodemus: Prominent member of the Sanhedrin, and a man of wealth; lived in Jerusalem in the first century C.E. [which means Common Era, or we would say AD]....In all probability he is identical with the Talmudical Nicodemus ben Gorion, a popular saint noted for his miraculous powers.[5]

Nicodemus was a member of the elite Jewish Sanhedrin, consisting of seventy men of great wealth and influence who judged in Israel. He would have also been of the Pharisee persuasion.

Christ told this already religious man that to enter the kingdom he must be, "born again" (John 3:3). In Greek the phrase *born again* is *gennao*, which means, "to procreate or to regenerate." The act of procreation brings forth a new living being who was never in existence before. To regenerate can mean to re-gene, or remove the old genes, replacing them with a new set of genes in the cells of the body. I would call this a spiritual *blood transfusion*, when the blood of Christ creates a new life causing old things to pass away. Nicodemus, a devout Jew, had been *physically* born through the watery womb of his mother. As a Pharisee he immersed frequently at the temple in a *mik'vot*, a hollowed-out baptismal-type pool with fresh rain or spring water. Men were required to submerge as a ritual purification before entering the temple compound. To enter the kingdom, repentance was required, something Nicodemus was familiar with, for each year on the Day of Atonement he and other devout Jews sought God for repentance and forgiveness.

At that time there were rabbinical thoughts on how someone could be "born again," which was a phrase for coming into salvation with the God of Israel. The eight ways were:

1. When a Gentile converted to the Jewish faith, moving from a Gentile to a Jew through conversion.

2. When a Jewish man was crowned a king, he was said to begin a new life or to be "born again."

3. By ritually purifying in the waters of the *mik'vot*; this purification was an act of being born again.

4. Repentance was the next level of being born again, which began a new life for the one repenting.

5. When a Jewish boy turned thirteen and held his *bar mitzvah*, moving into manhood, he was being born again.

6. Marriage was another new beginning from a single life to a husband, a type of being born again.

7. When a man reached thirty and took on rabbinical ordination, he was considered as born again.

8. If the man arose high to run a rabbinical school or teach students, his new life made him born again.[6]

The message of Jesus is that men are born of water first—being formed in the amniotic fluid of their mothers. Being born of the "spirit" was a new concept, as the spirit of a human enters the body at conception when the fetus is in the womb. Nicodemus questioned how he could go back into the watery womb of his mother to experience this new life and enter the kingdom (John 3:4). Believing on Christ, repenting of sin, and turning toward righteous living introduces a new life and beginning for the person seeking the born-again experience.

The Hebrew word link between the *womb* of a woman (*rechem*) and mercy (*racham*) should reveal to us that we were born once in the womb of a woman, but we are born again in the womb of mercy—the mercy of God and His grace. Whenever a newborn infant's umbilical cord is cut, a new life begins outside the mother's womb. When a sinner is born again through mercy, that person is "born again," and a new creation in Christ (2 Cor. 5:17).

For any mother who is pregnant, you must dedicate your bloodline to the Lord while the child is still in the womb. David wrote a Messianic prophecy in Psalms 22. These words can be applied to Christ, the Messiah:

> But You are He who took Me out of the womb;
> You made Me trust while on My mother's breasts.
> I was cast upon You from birth.
> From My mother's womb
> You have been My God.
> —Psalms 22:9–10

Spiritual leaders, kings, prophets, and even ministers are set apart for God's service from the wombs of their mothers. Jeremiah revealed:

Before I formed you in the womb I knew you;
Before you were born I sanctified you;
I ordained you a prophet to the nations.
—JEREMIAH 1:5

Isaiah also believed he was ordained to ministry from his mother's womb. He wrote: "Before I was born the LORD called me; from my mother's womb he has spoken my name" (Isa. 49:1, NIV). David knew that God was with him from before his physical birth, for he penned, "For You formed my inward parts; You covered me in my mother's womb" (Ps. 139:13). The apostle Paul was called to be an apostle by divine providence. He acknowledged this in Galatians, when he wrote, "But when it pleased God, who separated me from my mother's womb and called me by His grace, to reveal His Son in me" (Gal. 1:15–16).

Paul was a Pharisee and an enemy of the preaching of Christ and the Cross. Yet God had marked him while he was forming in his mother. Mothers, you never know the destiny you are carrying in your womb for nine months. God knows the future of your child, and perhaps this is why the battle is so intense before, during, and after the birth. You carry the seed in your womb, and the center of your spirit being is in the belly, for out of your belly flows the rivers of living water—the Holy Spirit Himself (John 7:38–39). Thus, when you travail in prayer, your prayer burden is birthed in the same area where your child was formed—out of the womb of mercy. Travail always precedes birth, and a heavy burden in prayer will always precede a spiritual breakthrough.

CHAPTER 7

PREPARING to BATTLE SEVEN END-TIME SPIRITS

SOME CONFLICTS ARE COMMON IN FAMILIES, JUST A part of life and raising kids with their siblings. Other conflicts emerge from seeds planted by the father or mother. More intense conflicts are motivated by spirits that are given an open door into a person's decision-making capabilities. David was a man after God's heart, but his heart strayed, impacting the hearts of his sons and causing family conflicts with Amnon, Absalom, and Adonijah.

His son Amnon lusted for his half-sister, eventually setting her up and raping her (2 Sam. 13:1–14), which, in the cultural setting of that day, defiled her, destroying her future destiny. His son Absalom became bitter toward his brother, wanting to kill him for raping his sister. Absalom did slay his brother, then left Jerusalem, thus avoiding his father's wrath (2 Sam. 13:23–37). A third son, Adonijah, rose up against his father's position as king, attempting a military coup, which was eventually crushed (1 Kings 1–2). The root causes of these family conflicts were *sexual immorality* (Amnon), *rebellion* (Absalom), and being influenced by the *wrong friends* (Adonijah). If we were to interview the average Christian family engaged in a clash with their teenage children today, these three issues would be the root of the battle: sexual immorality, rebellion, and being influenced by the wrong friends.

It should be noted that many of these family struggles began after David's affair with a married woman, Bathsheba, and the conspiracy to kill her husband in battle was publicly exposed. We know there was great disappointment in the kingdom with David when the sin was made known. David's disobedience made it difficult to discipline or instruct his sons, as they could bring up his past with rational arguments, such as, "You are telling me I am immoral…look at yourself," or "You don't want Amnon to receive judgment for raping my sister, when you had Bathsheba's husband killed?" The *deed* will always affect the *seed*, or your actions can come back to haunt you through your own children. If you have a smoking habit, it becomes a mockery to tell your kids, "Don't smoke because it's dangerous." If you drink your beer and wine in *private*, your children will drink in public, and your grandchildren could end up losing their driver's licenses and being charged with manslaughter from driving drunk. As a parent, you should live your life in such a manner as to never need to apologize to your children for what they saw you doing or heard you saying.

Seven Spiritual Forces

The first law of warfare is to know whom or what you are dealing with. I believe there are seven different types of spirits or spiritual forces assigned to distract, disrupt, and destroy this generation.

1. The spirit of deception

Prophetic students often refer to Matthew 24 when listing signs of Christ's return. We have all heard of wars, famines, and earthquakes. However, in this single chapter the strongest warning is against "deception," found four times in the one chapter (Matt. 24:4, 5, 11, 24). The Greek word for *deceive* means, "to wander or go astray from the truth." Jesus warned of the deception from men and false Christs (vv. 4–5). False prophets would pull people astray with false signs (v. 11).

At times I am amazed by how common deception is today, and how easily it is accepted when any type of rational argument is attached to it. One young man who smoked pot said he did so to concentrate better on Jesus. Another fellow said he drank lots of alcohol so he could better understand how to witness to drunks. That's as crazy as saying, "I need to commit adultery to know how to relate to all the adulterers out there."

Deception can be exposed only when the light of truth shines in the dark places. This generation is more ignorant of biblical knowledge than any before it. To pray against deception, one should pray that the eyes of a person's understanding will be opened to the truth (Eph. 1:18).

2. The spirit of seduction

Paul gave this warning when writing to Timothy:

> Now the Spirit expressly says that in latter times some will depart from the faith, giving heed to deceiving spirits and doctrines of demons, speaking lies in hypocrisy, having their own conscience seared with a hot iron.
>
> —1 TIMOTHY 4:1–2

We in America use the word *seduce* in connection with a woman sexually seducing a man or a man seducing a woman. The Greek word *seduce* is *planos* and refers to someone who is an *imposter or a misleader*. We could say it is a "misleading spirit," or a spirit that poses as an imposter to attract a person into a particular trap. For a spirit of this type to be successful in its assignment, it must tap into the emotional flow of an individual, as emotions are where all feelings reside. Sin without emotional feeling is like a sailboat without wind or a car without fuel. The boat and the car look good to the eyes but are useless for transportation.

There is a threefold result when following a seducing spirit: deception leading to false doctrine (doctrines of devils), lies being spoken with the knowledge they are lies, and self-deception from lying that eventually leads to an insensitive conscience. Under the spell of seduction, right is wrong, wrong is right, good is bad, and bad is good. To be released from this spirit, the darkness in the mind, heart, and spirit must be illuminated with the light of truth that will expose the lies and cause the person to see clearly. Usually after being freed from the stronghold of seduction, a person will comment, "I can't believe I didn't see that coming," or "How did I let that happen?"

3. The spirit of fainting

In Luke 18 in the parable of the steadfast woman, Christ taught that men ought to pray and "not to faint" (v. 1, KJV). There is a natural, emotional, and spiritual tiredness that can manifest in seasons. Natural weariness can come from overwork. Emotional tiredness can come from overextending yourself with the cares of life, and spiritual tiredness comes by being "weary in well doing" (Gal. 6:9, KJV).

Isaiah predicted that "Even the youths shall faint and be weary, and the young men shall utterly fall" (Isa. 40:30). The Hebrew word *fall* is *kashal*, and means, "to totter, to waver, and get weak in the legs." It is also translated as "cast down" (Jer. 6:15; 8:12). The younger generation of today is often considered lazy, as they sit around playing with the latest tech gadget. Actually their motivation is being sapped by the enemy and the tools he uses to snare our youth.

The solution to fainting and weakness is to "wait on the LORD," and He will "renew their strength" (Isa. 40:31). The word *wait* refers to binding together as in the sense of twisting twine together. The idea is not to be idle and sit around as though you are waiting for a phone call or the doorbell to ring, but indicates quality time in God's presence. If the joy of the Lord is your strength (Neh. 8:10), and in God's presence is fullness of joy (Ps. 16:11), the strength from the joy will overtake the spirit of fainting and weariness.

4. The spirit of rejection and shame

This generation has encountered and endured more *rejection* than any before it. One Greek verb for *reject* in Scripture is *apo-dokimazo*, meaning, "to examine and then to disapprove of." This is the word used when the priest and elders examined Christ and rejected Him, choosing for Him to die instead of releasing Him (Matt. 21:42; Mark 8:31).[1] The feeling of rejection begins in youths when they discover their mothers almost aborted them and their fathers did not want them. Later as children or early teens, they endure divorce, splitting the family in half. Seeking acceptance from outside the family, a mother's daughter goes from one relationship to another, one broken friendship to another, and at times moves from one location to a new one, living life in a dark hole feeling like a wind spinning in all directions and out of control.

Often youths will try to compensate for a feeling of rejection by forging unhealthy relationships and doing whatever is necessary or requested by "friends" to be accepted. This often leads to sexual immorality, drunkenness, drug abuse, and perversion, with the road ending in condemnation and shame. The Internet has been used to retaliate against a boy or girl by showing pictures or telling a story of that person's sin for all to see or read. Unable to deal with the shame, many youths have taken their own lives.

It is the responsibility of parents, ministers, and youth leaders to emphasize God's gift of redemption, which can remove condemnation and release a repentant sinner from the shame game. Isaiah noted:

> Instead of your shame you shall have double honor,
> And instead of confusion they shall rejoice in their portion.
> Therefore in their land they shall possess double;
> Everlasting joy shall be theirs.
> —ISAIAH 61:7

In place of reproach and humiliation God will give you a double inheritance, blessing, and reward. The word *confusion* refers to the blushing on a face because of the humiliation of being discovered in sin. While the primary application of this verse was addressed to the Jews returning from Babylon, the same spiritual application is valid for anyone coming out of Satan's bondage, sin, and prison house of death. God turns sorrow into joy, mourning into dancing, and gives a double blessing of peace and joy to a forgiven soul. Repentance leading to forgiveness is an amazing grace—as God does not remember your sins, and you are released from guilt and shame.

5. The spirit of distraction

There are three words making up this one word: *action*, *traction*, and *distraction*. Life is forever moving forward into the future. One second is right now, and one second that follows is the future. When one minute passes, we live in the *now* minute, looking ahead to the future minutes. The same is true with hours and days: the past, present, and future. Forward motion requires *action*, followed by *traction* to keep the momentum flowing. Bald tires will spin in the mud, but new tires will grip on to something beneath them, thrusting your vehicle out and forward. Distractions, however, impact your traction and your action.

I was once told that a person should plan at least 20 percent of a day for the unexpected and unplanned distractions. In business and family to be pulled away from scheduled plans to the unexpected hindrances is a norm. Spiritual distractions are designed to stop any forward progress—to *dis-track* you, or move you off track.

It requires mental discipline not to allow distractions to detour your focus. The greatest level of discipline I ever witnessed was in the United States Army soldiers who guard the Tomb of the Unknown Soldier in Arlington National Cemetery in Washington DC. These highly trained men are so mechanical and precise in every movement that they seem like preprogrammed robots. Surrounded by thousands of people each day, it is their eyes that are amazing. No action, activity, or comment from anyone in front of them can cause them to crack a smile, grin, laugh, or respond in any manner. I was thirteen years of age when for thirty minutes I watched this most amazing mental discipline I had ever seen.

A believer must learn to pick and choose their distractions. Unexpected visitors, phone calls, and other daily cares may require attention, but any person, circumstance, or event that pulls you away from your spiritual assignment must be properly dismantled and defeated. At times I refuse calls, visitors, or meetings for a later time of day, as the present assignment requires undivided attention. Discipline in discerning distractions is necessary to prevent a default in your day. The adversary will throw stumbling blocks of minor hindrances to pull you from the main battlefield. It is the old magician's trick of *watch my right hand*, to prevent seeing the activity in the left hand. Take on the important matters and turn the minor ones over to trusted friends or workers.

6. The spirit of mocking

Take serious warning signs that your child is being mocked and verbally bullied in school or among friends, because the spirit of mocking has sent youth over the edge.

Samson broke his Nazarite vow when he exposed the secret of his strength. Delilah's scissors were phase one of his humiliation, followed by the loss of his eyes and being chained to a grinding stone. The Philistines made sport of him (Judg. 16:25, KJV), meaning they were verbally harassing and mocking him. Mocking is part of the persecution plan laid out against believers who make public confessions of their faith. At Christ's trial Roman soldiers began smiting Him on the face, mocking Him, and demanding Him to reveal the names of the persons hitting Him, calling Him "the king of the Jews" (Mark 15:18–20). Even on the Day of Pentecost, with obvious supernatural manifestations visibly moving the multitude, some were "mocking" (Acts 2:13).

The enemy wants to mock your confession of faith, your testimony, and your faith by creating what appears to be the *opposite results* of what you are praying for. The famous evangelist Smith Wigglesworth's résumé was filled with hundreds of healing testimonials, yet Smith had a daughter who was deaf and was never healed by Smith's prayers. Skeptics of the healing ministry would mock Smith and question how he could claim miraculous answers to prayer and not "heal his own daughter."

Well-known pastors of large congregations have hosted seminars on marriage and witnessed their own wives walking out the door with another man or confessing to being unfaithful. Warm church members suddenly turn a cold heart as they criticize, "Their own wives didn't follow their preaching" or "What a hypocrite to teach one thing and live another way." The same is true when a mocking spirit arises against a youth minister who directs the college and career class at the church but has a child of his or her own who is in rebellion. Some well-meaning yet outspoken *saint* will comment, "What is he doing teaching the youth when he can't control his own child?"

Perhaps you have heard this subtle mocking voice questioning you. "How can you pray for the sick when you are suffering yourself?" "How can you speak on giving when you have nothing to give?" "How can you speak deliverance over others when you have a child on drugs?"

Satan is hungry for another trophy in his showcase giving him bragging rights in the spirit world. Job 1:8 reveals that God can boast to Satan about His faithful believers, and when the adversary gains the upper hand in the life of those created in God's image, he moves from an attacker to the accuser. Christ was mocked, but He knew the final outcome and got the last laugh.

7. The spirit of blindness

Consider the strong man Samson. Once the Philistines discovered the secret of his strength and cut his hair, Samson was weakened to the level of any normal man. The Philistines gouged out his eyes. There were other methods of inflicting punishment. Not to sound grotesque, but why didn't they remove his thumbs and big toes as Judah did to the captured king Adoni-Bezek (Judg. 1:4–6)? Why did they not remove his tongue so he could never speak again? Could they not have punished him by cutting off his ears so he could never clearly hear again? Why did they go after his eyes?

Without his eyes, Samson could never see foxes again and tie their tails together and burn their fields. Without his eyes, he could never again spot a donkey's jawbone on the ground and use it as a deadly weapon. A sightless champion is a helpless ex-hero who will never again be able to see who the enemy actually is. Is the voice speaking young or old, an enemy or a friend, an Israelite or a Philistine? The spirit of blindness disables the discernment of its victim. In the fog of confusion friends appear as enemies, and enemies become friends. To the spiritually blind, parental authority becomes control, spiritual warnings become tricks of manipulation, and dangerous actions become signs of their freedom to choose.

The spiritually blind are leading the spiritually blind, and Christ taught they will both fall in the ditch (Matt. 15:14). The eyes of understanding must be enlightened and then fully opened. One of the most important and continual prayers to pray is that the eyes of understanding will be opened to truth and received.

This list of seven different types of "spirits" that attack, influence, and attempt making inroads to impact a negative outcome of your circumstances, disrupting your life flow, can seem overwhelming—which is the motivation of their manifestations—to *wear you down* physically, emotionally, and spiritually, as the adversary's strategy is to wear us down. (See Daniel 7:25.) However, with each adversarial strategy there is a counterstrategy from the Lord.

God's simple tactical advantage provided for believers is found in the actions of two words: submit and resist. We read in James 4:7:

> But He gives more grace. Therefore He says: "God resists the proud, but gives grace to the humble."
> Therefore submit to God. Resist the devil and he will flee from you. Draw near to God and He will draw near to you. Cleanse your hands, you sinners; and purify your hearts, you double-minded.

The word *humble* in Greek is *tapeinos*, and refers to laying low. Humility is a magnet for God's favor, as God resists the proud and gives grave (favor) to the humble. The Greek word *submit* is *hupeiko*, and means "to retire or to withdraw." In this reference "submitting to God" refers to withdrawing from your own desires or will and completely giving yourself and all you have over to God for His pleasure and purpose. This is what Christ did in the garden when He requested that if it were possible let this cup (of suffering) pass from Him, yet not His will but God's will be done (Matt. 26:39). Often a person will submit to God, but they must also resist the devil.

The Greek word *resist* in James 4:7 is interesting, as it is the word *anthistemi*, from the word *anti*, meaning "against," and from *histemi*, meaning "to cause to stand." It means to stand against or to withstand. In classical Greek it meant for a soldier to get a strong footing and hold his ground without moving or giving an inch and resist the opponent. It also referred to taking a position that is one hundred eighty degrees opposite of what is being said, taught, or before a person. When Paul spoke of believers putting on the whole armor of God, three times he instructed that a believer must "stand" (Eph. 6:11, 13, 14). Paul taught we must "withstand in the evil day," and instructed the saints, "Having done all to stand, stand therefore." In all three verses the Greek word *stand* is the word *hestemi*, one of the words that makes up the word used for resist in James 4:7.

Christ was tempted of the devil for forty days. The adversary wanted Christ to perform miracles to prove His identity as God's Son. This included turning stones into edible bread and jumping off a high wall in Jerusalem in the belief that angels would come and protect Him, if He were God's Son. In three major temptations Christ resisted the devil and refused to take up any of his three offers (Matt. 4:1–10). The Word of God became a sword of the Spirit and a powerful weapon in the mouth of Christ to resist the antagonistic voice of the accuser. The Scriptures are today our sword of the Spirit, the Word of God, to resist the enemy (Eph. 6:17).

James warned about being "double minded" (1:8). This word

refers to being double soled or having a double opinion about one thing. It can mean for a person's mind to be split in half. Instead of taking a stand and resisting evil, when they are with believers they look, act, and talk like believers, but when they are working with people in the world, they act and converse with the same carnal language of the world. When asked if they believe something is a sin, if they are with Christians who believe it's wrong, then they agree it's wrong. But if asked the same question by a group of sinners, they may back up and say they don't see anything wrong with the particular activity. A double-minded person cannot receive anything from God (James 1:6–8).

Another point in this James discourse is where he said to "cleanse your hands" (James 4:8). If we have any sins that have not been confessed and forsaken, and we are abiding in unrighteousness, then spiritually our hands are defiled. The easiest way for the adversary to get into our lives, bringing any one of these seven spirits against us, is through spiritual cracks in the door that are opened with a sin key. Don't just think of sins being lying, stealing, murder, or adultery. Believers have their own black book of secret sins that they like to ignore and gloss over, such as anger, bitterness, jealousy, and unforgiveness.

If we will confess and forsake our sins and iniquities, submit to God and resist the devil, then the adversary and all his cohorts must flee (literally run away) from us. These seven end-time spirits and mental temptations can be defeated in advance by submitting and resisting.

CHAPTER 8

WAITING LONG FOR AN ANSWER

SOME SHORT-WORDED PRAYERS GET ANSWERED IN A short time, and some long-worded prayers seem to require a long time. Peter said three words, "Lord, save me," and was immediately rescued from drowning (Matt. 14:30–31). Daniel prayed and fasted for three weeks before receiving the revelation for which he prayed (Dan. 10:3–12).

There are several biblical laws that guide a believer, which must not be broken to receive answers to prayer. First, *unforgiveness toward another person* can block the answer to your prayers (Matt. 6:14–15). Too much tossing to and fro creates uncertainty and mixes faith with unbelief, stopping the flow of answers from manifesting. This mix is like a wife crying out for God to save her marriage while she is driving to a lawyer she hired to file for divorce. When *wavering*, we sit on a fence of hope with one foot positioned on the side of belief and one foot on the side of doubt, leaning in one direction or the other. When a person prays and then wavers, they can't receive anything from God (James 1:6–8). James 1:6 in the 1611 King James reads, "Let him ask in faith, nothing wavering."

There are two different Greek words translated as wavering. One is found in Hebrews 10:23, where we are told to "hold fast the confession of our faith without wavering," which means "without blending or mixing." The word in James means ask in faith and *do not withdraw* from your belief and do not *stagger* or doubt.[1]

When we pray directly in faith, followed up by such comments as, "I don't know if God heard that" or "I'm about to quit and give up because nothing is happening," then our *double-minded* wavering has moved from our heads to our mouths. From a practical application, many have a *lack of expectation* that what they are praying will soon become answered prayer. This lack of expectation reminds me of when the early saints prayed all night for Peter to be released from prison. The angel unlocked his chains and the prison doors and the iron gates to the city, releasing Peter to attend his own prayer meeting! When those inside heard Peter's voice through the door, they were in shock that what they believed for had occurred (Acts 12:5–10). They had *faith* but not *expectation*.

There is also a spiritual application as to why at times answers are delayed. Spiritual authority is increased when others join in agreement. Being raised in a full-gospel denomination, I saw older believers grouped in small rooms in rural churches, pouring out their souls toward the heavens. This generation of prayer warriors is passing away, meaning if they are not replaced, when they pass on their prayer space becomes a void. A declining generation of prayer teams leaves a weaker prayer base. Rooms that once shook the church with fifty praying individuals are now used for storage space.

With the influx of foreigners to America, bringing their gods and religious customs in their suitcases and in their hearts, all forms of idolatry open doors to evil spirits connected to the worship of false gods. In our own state of Tennessee one of the main Middle Eastern religions has leaders who have made public statements that they will one day control the state of Tennessee. In my own town of Cleveland one businessman who represents this religion made a statement that when a major denominational headquarters eventually shuts its doors, he would step in and purchase it, turning it into a house of worship for his (non-Christian) religion. This same religion is purchasing hundreds of churches that have closed and turning them into their own religious buildings. Spirits connected with other religions are clashing with the traditional American faith, which has been Christianity. These spirits impact the upper atmosphere like layers of air pollution, hindering believers when and where they can. (See Daniel 10:12–14 for the best example.)

The legalizing of abominations and permitting of evil brings a grieving to both the Spirit-filled believer and the Holy Spirit Himself. The Holy Spirit can be grieved by a believer's *internal conflicts* that lead to acting contrary to God's Word. Paul wrote, "And do not grieve the Holy Spirit of God, by whom you were sealed for the day of redemption. Let all bitterness, wrath, anger, clamor, and evil speaking be put away from you, with all malice" (Eph. 4:30–31). The Spirit is also grieved by the *external activities* of others, including the permitting and promotion of sins considered abominations. The man Lot was grieved by seeing the abominations and hearing the filthy conversations of the men in Sodom (2 Pet. 2:7).

The answer to your prayer hinges on your steadfast faith and patience to wait for God's response. The demonic activity increasing in America, and the level of abominations being permitted, can release the authority of demonic activity to levels previously unseen. The mental and spiritual pressure of these evil entities can bury a believer in oppressive vexation, that if not checked and removed will discourage the believer's persistence and move him or her to give up.

An intercessor will stand in the gap for another person or country. Prayer is intended to change circumstances and alter problems. Christ sent His disciples by boat to the other side of the Sea of Galilee. At the fourth watch (3 a.m.) Christ was praying when He knew His disciples were in danger in the middle of the lake.

> And when He had sent them away, He departed to the mountain to pray. Now when evening came, the boat was in the middle of the sea; and He was alone on the land. Then He saw them straining at rowing, for the wind was against them. Now about the fourth watch of the night He came to them, walking on the sea.
>
> —MARK 6:46–48

In the entire narrative there are three important requirements to bringing Christ into the storm and leading the disciples to safety: *perception*, *interception*, and *intervention*.

This first requirement is *perception*. In the narrative it is dark (the fourth watch), and Christ is on a high mountain praying. Having been to this area more than thirty times, I know that you cannot see anything on the lake until after sunrise. Christ did not see them with His natural eyes, but He *perceived* in His spirit what was invisible to His sight. Another way of saying this is that Christ discerned His men were caught in a storm. When high winds blow on the lake, stirring high waves, they also crash against the high mountains and can almost knock a person off his feet if the pressure is strong enough.

The second act of this story was *interception*—meaning Christ interrupted the sudden storm with His presence. Normally it would take time to walk off the high mountain and walk to the middle of the lake. Here, however, the time required was removed, and instantly Christ went from the hidden prayer mountain to the center of the storm. He intercepted the crisis when His presence arrived. Often we speak of an unexpected storm striking our lives, when what we need is the presence of Christ to show up in the middle of the storm. His voice will alter the wind and waves—what is around us and beneath us.

Third, there was *intervention* when the presence of Christ was stronger than the storm, and with His words, "Peace be still," He brought calm where there had been fear. Intervention can only occur when the victim caught in the storm is willing to allow others to help, to let them step into the boat and help him or her row safely to the destination. When dealing with a person who is heavily addicted to drugs and alcohol, intervention is impossible as long as that person believes he can row his own ship into dangerous winds without sinking the boat and dying prematurely.

Three Significant Keys

For those desiring to become effective intercessors who see results from their prayers, there are three significant keys that must be understood and put into practice.

1. Praying early in the morning

Jesus rose up a great while before day, meaning before sunrise, to pray. Scripture teaches it was the fourth watch, a Roman term referring to the time frame between three and six in the morning, right before the glow of the morning sun rises from the east, over the western mountains at the Sea of Galilee. The *practical* reason He prayed at this time was that the multitudes of people were sleeping, and Christ could have solitude between Him and the Father. The spiritual reason may have been the fact that the demonic spirits working in the spirit world must have people to work and speak through, and thus with everyone asleep, there was limited activity in the spirit realm.

However, there are numerous references to angelic activity occurring at *night* and just before sunrise. We know that angels of God are commissioned on special assignments at night, indicated by two angels in Sodom working *before sunrise* to get Lot's family out of the city (Gen. 19:1–23). Jacob wrestled an angel all night, right up until the sun arose (Gen. 32:24). It was at night when God sent an angel through the camp of the Assyrians, delivering Jerusalem by slaying one hundred eighty-five thousand enemy soldiers at once (2 Kings 19:35). Joseph received a dream of an angel while sleeping, telling him to take Mary as his wife (Matt. 1:20), and an angel came from heaven ministering strength to Christ in Gethsemane, late at night, before He was arrested (Luke 22:43). Christ was resurrected just before sunrise, meaning that the angels were at the tomb just before the light of day (John 20:1; Matt. 26:45). When Peter was arrested in Jerusalem, we read, "But at night an angel of the Lord opened the prison doors and brought them out" (Acts 5:19). Peter was visited by a delivering angel at night, waking him from his sleep and releasing him from prison (Acts 12:6–10).

Releasing angelic messengers at night may be centered around the times known as the "night watches," a set time known in both the Old and New Testament periods. David wrote in Psalms 63:6: "When I remember You on my bed, I meditate on You in the night watches." The Jews set three night watches—from sunset to ten o'clock (four hours), from ten to two o'clock (four hours), and from two to sunrise (four hours), totaling a twelve-hour period; as Christ indicated there were twelve hours in a day (John 11:9). Whenever David awakened during the night, his focus was upon the Lord during the time of the night watches. Job revealed that God spoke to men in the night when deep sleep overtakes them (Job 33:15–19). This fact is evident with Daniel and Zechariah, both of whom saw visions at night (Dan. 7:2, 7, 13). David wrote that God gave him instruction in the night (Ps. 16:7), and that God visited him in the night (Ps. 17:3).

At Jerusalem (and walled cities) there were watchmen appointed to stand watch on top of the walls to watch for any invading enemies or messengers traveling at night, as the gates of the city were shut and locked at sunset, providing protection from night thieves (Obad. 5) or unwanted individuals. Watchmen also announced the arrival of the morning with the sunrise, and the coming of night with sunset (Isa. 21:12).

The New King James Bible uses the word "watcher" (Dan. 4:13), and "watchers," to describe a type of angels:

> This decision is by the decree of the watchers,
> And the sentence by the word of the holy ones,
> In order that the living may know
> That the Most High rules in the kingdom of men,
> Gives it to whomever He will,
> And sets over it the lowest of men.
> —DANIEL 4:17

This section of Daniel was written in Aramaic, thus the word "watchers," which is 'iyr from the Chaldean Aramaic, means properly a watcher, but refers to be hot and ardent; then to be lively, or active; and then to awake, to be awake, to *be awake at night, to watch*. The word used here is employed to denote one who watches, and in these places evidently applied to the angels, but *why* this term is used is unknown.[2] The idea of celestial angels being watchers over the cosmos and the souls of men was known in Babylon and among the Persians in the time of Daniel. Even other religions in the day believed there were four watchers over the four regions of the earth. They were Tashter who guards the east, Statevis watches the west, Venant the south, and Haftorang the north.[3]

In the Chaldean tradition specific angels are assigned during the night to watch and guard men. When Jacob wrestled the angel all night, the angel demanded Jacob to let him go, "for the day breaks" (Gen. 32:26), meaning the sun was soon to rise in the east. This angel had been assigned in the night to watch over Jacob, and there would be a *shift change* coming in which this angel was required to be back in the heavenly temple before the sun was seen on earth.

When considering the theme of praying early in the morning, there is always increased sinful activity and demonic activity during the time of sunset until late into the night. However, during the fourth watch, about three in the morning, although human activity ceases, roads in the city become empty, the air is silent from conversations, there are angels actively engaged in their ministry assignments. Praying early before sunrise can possibly release the ministry of a watcher on your behalf.

2. Praying a full sixty minutes

Great intercessors always pray for a longer time than the average believer prays. When my father was living, he would often come by my office and his first words to me would be: "Brother, do you want to have a word of prayer?" I knew that it was best for me to set aside lots of time, because he never prayed a short, brief prayer. When he traveled with me and we roomed together, one hour of prayer was as common as eating a main meal a few hours before service.

I once heard of a professor at a Christian university who commented in his class that it was useless to pray longer than five to ten minutes a day. His theology was based upon his opinion and not on the pattern of Christ. When Christ began interceding in Gethsemane, it is understandable that He would pray three hours because He was soon to face death and become the sin offering for mankind. However, He rebuked His disciples for sleeping when He said, "Could you not watch with Me one hour?" (Matt. 26:40). In this instance they, not an angel, were assigned to be the watchmen and to listen to His words. Had Peter heard Christ's words instead of sleeping, he would have never cut off the ear of the high priest's servant because he would have known that the events were a God setup.

Many believers use the excuse that they are *too busy* to pray for one hour. I suggest they take a notepad and write down how much time they spend in one day watching television, spending time on the Internet, or social networking on Facebook. It is not that people *don't have* time; it is that they *are not making time* because prayer is not a priority with them. A two-hour Sunday morning service satisfies their spiritual appetite, and the rest of the time is for work, sleep, eating, and personal activities.

Great intercessors understand the power of a sixty-minute prayer time. Having rubbed shoulders with powerful prayer warriors during my entire lifetime, I understand that one of the reasons they can spend extended time praying is because they mix their prayer with different types of prayer. Often they begin praying in their *native language*, English in this case. Then they move from praying with their understanding (English) to praying in the prayer language of the Holy Spirit, which is *praying in other tongues* (1 Cor. 14:14–15). Their prayers of petition are eventually turned into *thanksgiving and worship*. Eventually speaking words turns into *singing words* as the intercessors speak to themselves in psalms, hymns, and spiritual songs (Eph. 5:18–19). Depending upon the level of the prayer burden, the intercessor may move from praying words of understanding to what the Bible describes as "groanings, which cannot be uttered" (Rom. 8:26). The idea of groaning does not refer to the *content* of the prayer, but rather the *intensity* of prayer. The believer who engages in groaning is usually under spiritual distress or a heavy burden. When slavery in Egypt became unbearable, the Hebrews began to cry out to God with groaning (Exod. 3:7; Acts 7:34). The groaning revealed their intense longing for deliverance—deep sighs rising out of their human spirits, too deep for human words to explain (Rom. 8:26). It should be understood, however, that groaning is a language God understands.

3. Following the burden

In the New Testament there are several different Greek words translated as "burden" in English. One can refer to a physical load, such as cargo on a ship (Matt. 11:30). Another refers to a mental weight or load that weighs a person down (Acts 15:28). A third meaning is a weight or burden one person imposes upon another (2 Cor. 12:16).

Throughout life, believers who are spiritually inclined and tuned in to God's spiritual frequencies can pick up signals of impending danger or the hoofbeats of a coming satanic attack. God is aware of conversations and decisions being made in the spirit realm, and can reveal the battle plans before the war, just as God gave inside information to Elisha of the secret plans of the Assyrians before they arrived on Israel's soil. (See 2 Kings 6:8–20.)

It is these internal weights or pressure that bring a believer to his or her knees in prayer. In previous books and in live messages I have shared how about one week prior to a relative or a close friend dying, I come under a heavy weight that becomes unbearable, usually sending me home from the office to pray alone in my bedroom. This strange feeling has preceded the departure of about ten different people. To me, it is a signal to prepare for someone close to leave us. Those in the secular world would call this a *premonition*. These spiritual weights can be misread or missed if a receiver is too busy with the cares of life to take the time to discern the internal pressure.

Be careful not to misread the burden as mental or spiritual depression or oppression, although they can often feel the same. The difference is that oppression and depression are often triggered by specific circumstances or fear of the future, causing the mind to become filled with negative images and the mouth filled with negative words. However, a spiritual burden comes suddenly and often without the person bearing it knowing for whom or what they are praying. True intercessors accept burdens as God's signal to transition from normal activity to a position of prayer.

Feeding the Wrong Spirits

Christ told Peter to feed His sheep and His lambs (John 21:15–17). Paul wrote to feed the church of God (Acts 20:28), and Peter said to "feed the flock" (1 Pet. 5:2, KJV). Baby Christians must have the simplicity of the milk of the Word, and strong believers require the meat of the Word (Heb. 5:12–13). The words of Christ are spirit and life—spirit in that they impart life to the human spirit and energize the inward man.

Just as the human spirit must be nourished to be strengthened spiritually, demonic powers feed off the sins of the flesh and become stronger in the life of an active sinner. One of the most common doors that keeps the adversary energized is the spirit of fear (2 Tim. 1:7). Growing up I was told that if you step on a crack it can break your mother's back. People today still dread Friday the thirteenth or resent staying on the thirteenth floor of a hotel. A black cat crossing your path is supposed to bring bad luck, and in my day you avoided walking under a ladder. No one ever explained who came up with these ideas that maintained these phobias from generation to generation, but these are simple examples of how fear controls the imagination. Your inner spirit can be full of faith or full of unbelief, full of faith or fear, full of joy or depression, depending upon the type of *food thoughts* you are feeding it.

Feeding off your unbelief

Any type of spiritual unbelief, whether in your spirit, mind, or words, is food that feeds the enemy. Unbelief will stop all blessings of God from flowing in your direction. The entire spirit world can discern if you really believe or if you are in doubt. When Christ's disciples attempted to cast an evil spirit out of a boy with epilepsy, their unbelief became a roadblock, allowing the spirit to remain in the lad unchallenged. Jesus took complete authority over the infirm spirit by demanding it to depart. After the miracle the spiritually defeated disciples questioned why their prayers had failed. Jesus said, "Because of your unbelief" (Matt. 17:20).

Unbelief strengthens evil spirits, and faith reduces their grip. I have also learned that demons can detect the willingness of a person to either hang on to them or to let go of them. This is the greatest challenge for a parent who is praying for a child or, for that matter, praying for anyone who is resisting the gospel of deliverance. The human will can *submit* or *resist*, but seldom does it remain *neutral*. A neutral will of indecision prevents that person from going to the left or to the right, causing the person to remain stuck where he is.

Neither you nor I can force a conversion upon anyone. I get amused when hearing liberal talking heads in the *blame-stream media* always blaming conservatives, especially Christians, for the nation's troubles. When a Christian speaks openly of his or her faith, these fear mongers begin screaming, "They are forcing their faith upon people," as they desperately try to paint an image of a Christian holding someone down and pouring God pills down the throat. The fact is, it is impossible in a free society to force anyone to believe in anything they choose not to believe in; they have a will to believe or not.

For a parent who is praying for the salvation of a strong-willed child or marital partner, how can you pray in confidence knowing the person has no desire to be saved and only resents your intercession for him or her? By experience this is where you must pray for one of three things to occur:

1. The breaking of their will

2. The changing of their will

3. The forsaking of their will

After many years of full-time ministry and traveling, I know that it requires intense intercession when seeking for a person's will to be broken. You must discern what are the person, thing, or circumstances keeping that person from a redemptive covenant. Soul ties to wrong people, addictions to drugs, or just the love for the pleasure of sin can be three strongholds chaining that person's will to fleshly desires. Once you know the root source, then pray that the stubbornness of their will be broken. This answer can come in the form of a negative relationship being severed, a bad or near-death experience from drugs, or the person becoming sick and tired of living sick and tired.

At other times we can pray for the changing of the person's will. For example there are numerous men who are moral in their character, but they have no desire to serve the Lord or attend church. These individuals need a change in their will; a change from no desire for God to a desire for God. This change of will and change of choosing often occurs after a man is married and becomes a father. Knowing that a new life is in his hands and will be watching his lifestyle is a responsibility that causes him to see the need to raise his child in faith. The wife of one of my staff members had several miscarriages when her husband was still without God. When she became pregnant again and there was a bad report early in the pregnancy, he began believing that it was his lifestyle causing the miscarriages and that once again he would lose a child. This circumstance caused him to radically turn his life over to Christ, and the child, a girl, became a miracle baby and is today a lovely young woman.

The third prayer is that a person will forsake his will or ways and choose the way of God. The meaning of the word *repent* is not only, "to be sorrowful for wrong," but it also means, "to change directions." Your willpower is the rudder on the ship. When the rudder turns, the boat will turn. When a person forsakes his or her own will and follows God's, then the rudder of choosing faith will steer the vessel of your life in the direction where the wind of the Spirit is blowing.

Feeding off of rebellion

The third food that feeds spirits is clearly rebellion. Solomon wrote:

> An evil man seeks only rebellion;
> Therefore a cruel messenger will be sent against him.
> —PROVERBS 17:11

We know rebellion when we see it in a person; it caused that person to respond the opposite of what he or she is instructed to do. However, is rebellion a spirit, an emotion, or an attitude? The answer is that it can be all three. As the first rebel, Satan was able to direct a third of the angels in a heavenly rebellion against God. His rebellion was rooted in pride, thus the root of rebellion is pride, and not just resistance.

During my years of ministry, I have met many people who walk in rebellion against spiritual authority, thinking they have the right information and that everyone else is wrong. Often if they are youth, the root of the rebellion is a negative event that occurred in the family—divorce, division, contention, strife, or confusion in general. In Hebrew the root word for *rebel* is *marah* and means, "to make bitter," as in the example of the bitter waters of Marah (Exod. 15:23). Bitterness begins as a root in the spirit. Any root that is planted will eventually grow, and in this case, it produces the fruit of bitterness.

Feeding off your wounds

Our ministry supports the Women of Hope, an addiction recovery program for women here in Cleveland. Their life stories tell what brought each of them to the edge of destruction—it was a series of wounds caused by people they trusted: molestation by a family member, rape by a boyfriend, divorce, and fighting in the family. The enemy knows how to capitalize on a person's wounds. Some are self-inflicted wounds that come through wrong choices. Solomon wrote:

> Whoever commits adultery with a woman lacks
> understanding;
> He who does so destroys his own soul.
> Wounds and dishonor he will get,
> And his reproach will not be wiped away.
> —PROVERBS 6:32–33

Solomon's mother, Bathsheba, had an affair with King David as a married woman. No doubt while growing up Solomon heard the whispers, and many friends turned against David when they discovered his affair and slaying of the woman's husband in battle. Solomon wrote a warning to his son about strange women who

121

flatter young men with their words, saying that their attraction was like fire taken inside your bosom. (See Proverbs 6:23–33, KJV.) In Proverbs 6:33 the Hebrew word *wound* is *nega*, meaning, "a blow, a stain like leprosy on a person." Unless healed, a leper carries the scars of leprosy throughout his life, and Solomon knew from his father, David, that this type of sin carries long-term wounds. The chronicler writing the Book of 1 Kings notes this about David:

> Because David did that which was right in the eyes of the LORD, and turned not aside from anything that He commanded him all the days of his life, except in the matter of Uriah the Hittite.
>
> —1 KINGS 15:5

The good of David totally outweighed any bad in David's life. However, three thousand years later, when ministers speak of David—the man after God's own heart, the giant killer, the sweet psalmist and worshipper—the name of Bathsheba and his affair still remains in his résumé. Yet David held on to his personal faith in God, believing he would again see the *goodness* of the Lord in the land of the living (Ps. 27:13).

Holding on to a Thread

Using the analogy of Rahab's scarlet thread, there are ways in which the red thread applies to our prayer lives and families. I once saw a picture of a small kitten with both paws hanging on to the bottom of a rope. A caption read, "When you don't know what to do, tie a knot in the rope and hang on." The red thread of Rahab was a visible token to represent her family covenant with the Hebrew God. The scarlet cord had to remain placed in the window. She didn't pull it down, wave it around, run through the house shouting with it in her hands, or lay it on a table and pray over it. It was a sign of her covenant, and she never moved it from its rightful position.

For us the Bible is the Word of God and promises of our covenant. We can take a Bible and put it on a table, grab it, and run through the house, or even polish the cover. However, the Bible is just a Bible until it is read, believed, and hidden in our heart. The *promise* was in the red thread, but the *power of protection* was in the covenant. The Bible conceals the promises, but the power to activate them is released from the heart and mouth of a believer in covenant with God and Christ.

At times you will feel you have reached the end of your rope with no visible manifestation of your prayers being answered. This is when your faith is hanging by a thread.

There will be other times when you must use your faith for someone who is out of faith or not walking in covenant. It is like a person on the deck of a cruise ship seeing a person fall into the water and suddenly throwing them a life jacket or a life preserver. When a person is treading in water, surrounded by waves, and sees a flotation device, his desire for life will cause him to reach out and seize any object that will preserve him from a watery grave.

When you are standing in the emergency room of a child or close loved one who has taken an overdose or been in an unexpected car accident, or, as in one case I know, the person was shot by being in the wrong place at the wrong time, you must have that one thread—one covenant promise to hold on to.

Years ago when flying back from Madisonville, Kentucky, in a 421 twin-engine plane, I needed a scarlet thread to sustain my faith. My pilot and I were fifteen thousand feet in the air and about twenty minutes from the Chattanooga airport when the right engine suddenly went out. Neither the pilot nor I knew why, and we didn't know if the left engine would stop next, leaving us with an impossible landing and the chances of crashing in the night. What does a person do but pray for God's help? I had recently taught that Christ defeated Satan's premature death attacks by knowing God had a divine plan for His future. I began thinking of ministry promises God had made me and important assignments He revealed to me over the years that He desired for me to complete—most of which were not complete. I was in the beginning of a building project that I knew the Lord would have me build. I thought, "I can't die in a plane crash as there is too much for me to do that I haven't finished!" My faith surged, and I held on to that word. We made it safely to the airport. My scarlet thread was the many promises that were yet to be fulfilled.

Your scarlet thread could be a dream, a vision, a recorded word from the Lord in your journal, or a promise hidden in your heart. Noah required one hundred years to enter the ark and ride out the Flood. Abraham's vision was fulfilled twenty-five years after his first promise. Joseph spent thirteen years in prison, seven years preparing for famine, and two years into the famine—twenty-two years—before his brothers bowed down and his dream as a teenager unfolded before his eyes.

Living in the last days, which is the time prior to the return of Christ, is an interesting enigma. On one hand, there is a unique blessing predicted for this generation: the Holy Spirit will be poured out (Acts 2:17–18). On the other hand, the spiritual resistance from demonic rebels and hindering spirits will escalate. This tug-of-war is won by identifying the specific enemy opposing you, exposing it, and using weapons in your spiritual arsenal to drive out the spirit or spirits, replacing the void with the Word and the Holy Spirit.

CHAPTER 9

WHAT CAN YOU DO WHEN YOU ARE ALREADY UNEQUALLY YOKED?

THE UNITING OF A MAN AND WOMAN AS ONE FLESH was the first biblical covenant and commandment given by God in the garden to Adam and Eve: "Then God blessed them, and God said to them, 'Be fruitful and multiply; fill the earth and subdue it'" (Gen. 1:28). The marital covenant is one of the greatest physical, emotional, and spiritual blessings, especially when you find that one person whom God designed specifically to fit you. However, at times people marry and form marital bonds before their conversion, or one of the two partners—the wife or the husband—is not in covenant with Christ. This unequal balance has been a source of strife and division in homes from the beginning of the Christian faith. What can a dedicated Christian do when he or she is yoked with someone who is a firm unbeliever?

Paul wrote:

> Do not be unequally yoked together with unbelievers. For what fellowship has righteousness with lawlessness? And what communion has light with darkness? And what accord has Christ with Belial? Or what part has a believer with an unbeliever? And what agreement has the temple of God with idols?
>
> —2 CORINTHIANS 6:14–16

In this context Paul is writing to the believers in Corinth, Greece, a pagan city saturated in idolatry (2 Cor. 6:16). Paul was instructing believers to separate from the workers of darkness and have no association with them (v. 17). Paul compared the fellowship of a believer and an unbeliever to light trying to mix with darkness and of Christ being connected to Belial, a name for a spirit of wickedness. When believers fellowship with unbelievers, they can be tempted to revert back to sins of their flesh, pulling them back into the spiritual prison they were delivered from. Paul wrote:

> Stand fast therefore in the liberty by which Christ has made us free, and do not be entangled again with a yoke of bondage.
>
> —GALATIANS 5:1

In this context being "yoked" is a metaphor for associating with a person whose spiritual beliefs are opposed to the Christian faith. In Moses's law it was forbidden to yoke an ox and a donkey together (Deut. 22:10). Writing of the "unequal yoke" Paul may be using a metaphor from this law in his instruction. In the entire context Paul is warning about trying to yoke two opposites together—the temple of God with idols, righteousness with unrighteousness, light with darkness, and the table of devils with the cup of the Lord. Like oil and water, these opposites don't mix.

Paul's warning of the unequal yoke has been quoted by ministers for centuries to warn potential brides and grooms to choose a companion who is a believer and not marry outside the faith. A natural farm yoke connects two animals together for the purpose of work. If two animals wearing the same yoke are pulling in opposite directions, no work gets done, just as a husband and wife pulling in opposite directions will divide the peace, unity, and love required for a strong home and family.

Not all couples were believers when they were married. Some couples married when both were unsaved and now one is a believer and the other remains an unbeliever. Some entered marriage with one partner a Christian and the other unconverted. Occasionally two believers vow their lives together, and over time, because of acts of sin, one begins turning from the faith, dropping out of church, and becoming hardened of heart.

Five Different Types of Yokes

There are five possible types of yokes that a person can be connected to, with each one having its own negative impact.

1. Being yoked with *wrong friends* as a single person

2. Being yoked with the *wrong business partners* who operate in greed and selfishness

3. Being yoked with the *wrong type of religion* that is contrary to the Bible and the new covenant

4. Being yoked with the *wrong type of investments* and investors that end in a scam

5. Being yoked with an *unbeliever in marriage*

It would be wise for parents, even if you are a single mother, to provide early instruction for your children long before they consider marriage. In 1 Corinthians chapter 7 Paul gave wisdom and advice for believers who were unmarried. A young unmarried believer can focus all his or her attention on the work of God and involvement in ministry. Being married requires balancing a strong spiritual life with the daily cares of providing for the marital responsibilities and raising their family (vv. 32–34).

The instructions for the married are given in 1 Corinthians 7:12–16:

> But to the rest I, not the Lord, say: If any brother has a wife who does not believe, and she is willing to live with him, let him not divorce her. And a woman who has a husband who does not believe, if he is willing to live with her, let her not divorce him. For the unbelieving husband is sanctified by the wife, and the unbelieving wife is sanctified by the husband; otherwise your children would be unclean, but now they are holy. But if the unbeliever departs, let him depart; a brother or a sister is not under bondage in such cases. But God has called us to peace. For how do you know, O wife, whether you will save your husband? Or how do you know, O husband, whether you will save your wife?

This section of Paul's letter covers the issue of a believer's spiritual response to being married to an unbeliever. If you are a person of faith and in covenant with God, and your companion has not received Christ but you have a good marriage, then you are to remain together. If an unbelieving partner departs because of your faith and commitment to Christ—and not because you have sinned—then you are released to allow them to depart. The converted wife (or husband) can be a covering for her children, and her (or his) dedication sets apart her family for Christ.

How can a believing wife "sanctify" her family? She brings in a holy conversation and lifestyle into the home and sets an example for her children. Paul's instruction to these Gentile believers at

Corinth was important, as the Jews believed that if the parents of a child were not Jewish proselytes, the child was born out of holiness. Also they believed that children born to heathen parents were only holy if the parents were Jewish proselytes before the birth of the child. Paul made it clear that if a husband who was a sinner had children with a wife who was a believer, the children were not born in sin because the faith of the mother set the children apart to her. If the unsaved man was faithful to his wife and provided for his children, then the woman was to remain with the man and not divorce him.

It was important for Paul to make this point. The unbelief of a partner is not a reason for divorce if both the husband and wife love each other. The believing wife can eventually win the husband to the Lord through living out her faith in front of her husband and children. The apostle Peter pointed this out in 1 Peter 3:1–6:

> Wives, likewise, be submissive to your own husbands, that even if some do not obey the word, they, without a word, may be won by the conduct of their wives, when they observe your chaste conduct accompanied by fear. Do not let your adornment be merely outward—arranging the hair, wearing gold, or putting on fine apparel—rather let it be the hidden person of the heart, with the incorruptible beauty of a gentle and quiet spirit, which is very precious in the sight of God. For in this manner, in former times, the holy women who trusted in God also adorned themselves, being submissive to their own husbands, as Sarah obeyed Abraham, calling him lord, whose daughters you are if you do good and are not afraid with any terror.

It is very important that a Christian wife submits to her husband and does not resist him or, as we say, "rag on him," because of his lack of faith or unbelief. I have seen where a Christian woman would literally yell and verbally abuse her unsaved husband in the name of taking spiritual authority over him, and this action brought resentment to the Christian faith—as the husband blamed Christ for turning his wife into an outspoken critic of him and others like him. For a man it just does not work for his wife to hold his hand crying for his soul one minute, and then slap his hand in disapproval and yell at him the next minute. The wife must be stable and committed to the marriage covenant, knowing that tens of thousands of husbands have turned from unbelief to faith through the prayer and lifestyles of their believing wives.

Physical Relations Are Not a Weapon

A carnally minded woman will use the marital act or physical relations to retaliate against her husband when he acts in a manner that displeases her. I am not speaking here of a woman submitting to a drunken, physically abusive relationship, but of using the marital bed to manipulate her husband into doing what she wishes, or punishing him by closing the door to his desire of intimacy. Paul made it quite clear that withholding sexual benefits in a marriage will open a door to Satan:

> Do not refuse and deprive and defraud each other [of your due marital rights], except perhaps by mutual consent for a time, so that you may devote yourselves unhindered to prayer. But afterwards resume marital relations, lest Satan tempt you [to sin] through your lack of restraint of sexual desire.
> —1 CORINTHIANS 7:5, AMP

There are some practical applications to keep any marriage exciting, especially as a husband and wife age. A Christian woman's spirituality is no excuse to dress as a Victorian model in front of your husband. Having a house full of children is no excuse to cease from your covenant obligations to meet his (or her) physical needs. Your spirituality is not a cover to excuse a person's lack of taking care of herself (or himself) physically and at five in the afternoon looking like you just stepped out of bed. Paul even taught that if two believers choose to set aside a season for fasting and prayer, they should do so and come back together to perform the natural functions of marriage, lest Satan take an advantage of you and bring temptation.

As a word of encouragement, I have personally known of many Christian women who were married to good moral men who cared and provided for them. However, these men for different reasons never attended church or supported the ministry. As the wife remained a faithful companion and time passed, she won her husband to Christ with her determination and by being a loving wife to him. The key is unwavering love. A man or woman can close their ears to the hymns and songs and preaching of a minister, never entering the door of local church. However, it is impossible to resist love. Love melts hard hearts like heat melts wax.

CHAPTER 10

FIVE CRAZY PRAYERS TO PRAY WHEN YOUR FAMILY IS IN TROUBLE

NOT ALL PRAYERS ARE THE SAME. PAUL WROTE FOR believers to be "praying always with all prayer and supplication in the Spirit" (Eph. 6:18). The meaning of this phrase can refer to praying in the spirit on all occasions with all kinds of prayers and to praying in line with the Holy Spirit's wishes. In the New Testament there is the prayer of agreement where two agree (Matt. 18:19), prayers of thanksgiving (Phil. 4:6), the prayer of binding and loosing (Matt. 16:19), and the prayer of faith (James 5:15). Two of the new covenant prayers include praying in the Spirit and praying with the understanding (1 Cor. 14:14–15). There are different types of prayers for different situations.

In the Scripture there are examples of what I call *crazy prayers* or crazy requests. When Moses asked Pharaoh when he should ask God to remove the frogs, the king answered, "Tomorrow!" He wanted one more night with the frogs (Exod.

8:7–10). When a group of youth mocked Elisha, calling him a bald head and commanding him to go up, the prophet cursed them. Immediately two female bears came from the woods and devoured forty-two of the mockers (2 Kings 2:23–25). Peter prayed that he could walk on water while everyone else wanted to sit in the boat (Matt. 14:25–30). One of the oddest requests was when a demon called Legion requested Christ to send him and several thousand demons to enter the bodies of two thousands pigs, driving the swine insane, as they ran down a cliff into the Sea of Galilee.

I believe that when we pray for the salvation of a loved one, we often pray too passively with vague words such as, "Lord, help them…Lord, touch them…Lord, bring them in…Lord, move upon them." Our words must be sharpened and as straight as an arrow in a bow. With such generalization the Lord may be asking us, "Help them with what? Touch them when? Bring them in where? Move upon them how?"

Five Specific Prayers of Faith

There are five very direct and specific prayers that when combined in faith have seen great results among those who need a redemptive covenant with God.

1. Pray for their soul and spirit to be awakened

Years ago in the early 1990s I was ministering on a Sunday morning in a rural church just outside of Cleveland, Tennessee. That morning my Israeli tour guide, Gideon Shor, was vising our home and attended the service with us, as I wanted to introduce him to the people. I do not recall my exact message that morning, but at the conclusion of the message I began with the altar invitation. For a brief moment I began to *pray in the Spirit*, which is a manifestation of the Holy Spirit. The altar service, as we say, "broke loose," and concluded with spiritual results for the kingdom of God.

Afterward my guide Gideon commented, "I understood the words you were saying when you were praying in that other language. You said, 'Awake, wake up people, it is time to awaken and get up.'" Picking up his Hebrew Bible, he said it reminded him of the words of the female judge Deborah. Running his finger from right to left he read this from the song of Deborah, "Awake, awake, Deborah! Awake, awake, sing a song! Arise" (Judg. 5:12).

The reason for a person awakening is that they are slumbering— spiritually sleeping or mentally sluggish. I have sat in churches observing the youth where it seems the church youth group is on two different tracks, as one group is at the front of the church, hands lifted, singing and worshipping, and others are sitting back, arms folded, slumped in a pew, counting off minutes, anticipating the noon final prayer so they can get out, turn on their phones or computers, and get back into their social networking rut. The enemy thrives off of sleeping saints. In the New Testament parable of the sower sowing the seed of the Word, a man's field was planted with good seed. However, while he *slept* the enemy snuck in and planted tare seeds that later grew up choking the good wheat (Matt. 13:24–27). When Samson fell asleep in the lap of Delilah, she cut off the source of his covenant by breaking his Nazarite vow (Judg. 16). The spiritual slumbering in the weak soul of a lost child must be broken.

Karen Wheaton is the spiritual mother and director of one of America's most dynamic youth and college ministries called The Ramp. On one occasion the parents of a young man struggling with addictions asked Karen to come to their house, go to their son's room, and pray for his deliverance. The young man was at work, as the parents knew the fellow would resent direct prayer if he were at home. I was with Karen on this occasion, and I heard her pray these words, "Awaken, awaken his spirit by the Spirit of God. Cause his spirit to come alive in Your presence, and bring him out of the darkness." I had never heard a person pray for another person's spirit to be awakened. Yet, this is exactly what was needed.

The first type of prayer to pray on behalf of a backslider or a family member who is living in spiritual darkness, bound by their own lust and desires, is to pray for their mind and spirit to awaken to the things of God and to His Word. Paul wrote it this way, "[That] the eyes of your understanding being enlightened" (Eph. 1:18). He also wrote:

> Awake, you who sleep,
> Arise from the dead,
> And Christ will give you light.
> —EPHESIANS 5:14

This awakening theme was considered a part of the Jewish custom of sounding the shofar during certain Sabbaths, new moons, and feasts days, especially the Day of Atonement. Maimonides conjectures that the call of the trumpet, especially in the month Tisri, in which the great Day of Atonement occurred, was designed to signify a special call to repentance, meaning, "You who sleep, arouse from your slumbers; search and try yourselves; think on your Creator, repent, and attend to the salvation of the soul."[1] The voice of an intercessor who stands in the gap becomes the bridge of prayer between heaven and hell and is like the sound of a mighty shofar, piercing the darkness and splitting the veil that darkens the understanding of the sinner.

2. Pray for a change in the person's desires

All people have *desires*, a word carrying many meanings, including "to wish for, wait and long for or to express a request or a petition," but in this instance it is a passion or desire that is contrary to the Scripture or harmful to the body, soul, and spirit of a person. Smoking is a habit that is motivated by a desire. Drinking alcohol is motivated by desire, and every form of sexual immorality is rooted in desires stirred by the fleshly nature of the carnal man.

Years ago Nancy Reagan, the wife of President Ronald Reagan, began an anti-drug campaign called "Just Say No." I remember seeing commercials on television, billboards, and radio ads encouraging the youth to "Just Say No." Years later evidence showed that the campaign did little or nothing to prevent or slow down drug use. It was noted that just telling people no is not a strong motivator to prevent taking drugs since the peer pressure is greater than the inner motivation to refuse taking drugs.[2] In one study a group of athletes were told to just say no to steroids, while another was taught the danger of taking steroids. A year later it was found that the athletes who were exposed to the danger of taking steroids took fewer drugs than those told to resist them by saying no.[3]

People are visual and respond to *images* more than just *information*. In 1987 one effective commercial campaign launched by the Partnership for a Drug-Free America was a man holding an egg, saying, "This is your brain." The egg is cracked and put in a hot frying pan while the voice comments, "This is your brain on drugs." It ends with the words, "Any questions?" *TV Guide* named this commercial one of the top one hundred ever produced.[4]

Perhaps you saw one of the most effective anti-smoking commercials ever made, with a woman from North Carolina named Terrie Hall. Terrie was a heavy smoker whose voice box had been removed after being diagnosed with oral and throat cancer. The ad showed her putting on a wig and false teeth while covering a hole in her throat with a scarf, warning people about the dangers of smoking. The ad was aired on television and received more than

3.4 million views on YouTube.[5] Terrie died in September 2013 in a hospital in Winston Salem, North Carolina, at age fifty-three.[6] Her very graphic and shocking video may have accomplished more in getting people to stop smoking than any single advertisement or campaign.[7]

For people to stop their habits or change their dangerous life-styles, there must come a change in their *desires* or cravings. People become as passionate for their habits and bondages as some are about their relationships with their companions. Look at the men and women who have given up their families, including children, to sustain a drug or alcohol habit. The second prayer to pray is that God will completely change the lustful or dangerous desires of the person. On a few occasions I was asked to pray for a person who wanted to quit smoking but was having difficulty. I would fervently pray for the Lord to take away the *desire* for nicotine (the root cause for the craving), and if they smoked again to allow the smoke to make then uncomfortable or even sick. On numerous occasions the prayer brought results and freedom for the seeker.

3. Bind the strongman

In Matthew 12:29 we read, "Or how can one enter a strong man's house and plunder his goods, unless he first binds the strong man? And then he will plunder his house." It is impossible for a person to enter a house and seize possessions (spoil), if the house is being guarded by a *stronger person* than the *invader*. In this verse the strongman is Satan and his demonic hordes that are intent on pos-sessing, controlling, and eventually destroying the house—or the body of a person they control. Strong spirits construct *strongholds*, like castles with bars, preventing the person from getting out and outside help from getting in.

Christ imparted authority to the individual believer. This authority is the same as if Christ Himself was speaking, praying, or commanding. We cannot exercise authority if we choose to be at peace with the negative situation. In Mark 5 a man from the area of Gadara became possessed with at least two thousand individual spirits. When Christ addressed the chief demon, the spirit identified itself as "Legion," saying, "We are many." This spirit was the *strongman* in charge of the other spirits. It was this strong spirit that petitioned Christ not to send the entire army of demons out of the region. After his request, we read, "All the demons begged Him, saying, 'Send us to the swine, that we may enter them'" (Mark 5:8–12).

Many times spirits will attempt to hide their presence and identities until confronted with the presence of the Lord. Just as the religious Pharisees became cantankerous when Christ taught, evil spirits become agitated when the anointing is manifest. Using spiritual authority, believers must *bind* the opposing spirits. This Greek word *bind* is used when reapers bind tares in bundles, casting them into a fire (Matt. 13:30). It was used when the king's servants bound the man without a proper wedding garment and cast him into outer darkness (Matt. 22:13). To bind is to forbid, thus binding the strongman is to forbid the adversary to take up room and residence, driving him out through prayer.

4. Pray for God to bring confusion to bad relationships

Years ago one of our youth became burdened for her sister who was living on the West Coast in an alternative lifestyle. The soul tie was like chains around her sister, and the emotional attachment to the woman was unbreakable. The sister came and said, "How should I pray when she is choosing to live this way, and I cannot pray to counter her will when she wants to live this way?"

I had a sudden inspiration come to me that we should come into agreement that there would be division and confusion rising up in this unbiblical and dangerous relationship. We came into agreement that there would be no peace in the relationship and such confusion would break out, leading to separation. The prayer took eighteen months to answer, but the sister began losing a desire to be with the other woman, and she eventually broke off the relationship and moved to begin a new life.

5. Pray against seed stealers

In Christ's parable of the farmer planting seed (a parabolic analogy for planting God's Word in your heart), the failure and success rate is not based upon the strength of the seed—as the seed of God's Word is incorruptible. (See Mark 4.) It is based on the condition of the receiver, the one within whom the seed has been planted. For a spiritual transformation to occur, the Scriptures, biblical teaching, and word from God must take root in the heart and begin to grow. In the parable the ultimate job of the enemy is to prevent the seed (of the Word) from taking root in the heart of the person who hears the Word.

This significant parable reveals the four main conditions of the human heart that are encountered when the Word of God is preached, or the seed of God's Word is planted into the minds of the audience:

The Ground	The Condition of the Heart	The Result to the Person
The wayside ground	The hardened heart	No spiritual life
The stony ground	The rootless heart	A superficial life
The thorny ground	The worldly heart	A strangled life
The fruitful ground	The righteous heart	A successful, fruitful life

Some hear the preached Word, and the message *goes in one ear and comes out the other*. Others experience sitting under powerful biblical preaching and *become offended* at the teaching, thus what is being taught produces resentment instead of revival. Occasionally in my own ministry I have seen people walk out of a service when they disagreed with a point in the message. Others became excited for a short period, but eventually worldly distractions and the cares of life overwhelmed them to the point of choking the strength from their spiritual progress. Soon they were working overtime to pay bills, attended church very little, and seldom if ever supported God's work through tithes or offerings. The fourth group hears, receives, and acts upon the Word in faith. These 25 percent (or one in four according to the parable) are the believers who will receive a return on their spiritual investment, some thirty, some sixty, and some one hundred.

These scriptures on sowing the seed are often quoted when a minister is receiving an offering in a local church or encouraging believers to *plant a seed* into a project. The *soil* is considered the ministry. However, in the truest sense of interpretation the soil is the condition and receptivity of the person's heart receiving the seed of the Word. When a truth is read from Scripture or released from the pulpit, the hearer must plant the revelation being taught in the chambers of his or her mind, heart, and spirit. If this heart is not guarded, the persecution, pressure, circumstances, and negative people will rip out what was planted.

Throughout my ministry I cannot count the times when young people from nominal mainline churches would attend a conference and receive the baptism of the Holy Spirit. The moment they informed a friend or their pastor, they were told that what they received was not real, and they were warned they must not go back to the meeting but return to their own churches. Some would return, but others would not. The difference was that some did not have any depth of teaching on the Holy Spirit, and thus accepted the theological interpretation—based on unbelief—from their friends. Others had good seed planted that had already taken root, and no one could convince them that transformation in their lifestyles and the peace and joy in their spirits were not from the Lord.

If you have children who are high school teens or college age, often peer pressure from the opinions of friends will begin reaching in to rip out the seed you have planted in their spirits from an early age. You must pray against the seed eaters, the people and spirits assigned to weaken the soil of their hearts, preventing a fruitful life.

CHAPTER 11

REDISCOVERING YOUR KINGDOM AUTHORITY OVER LIVING THINGS

W E IN THE WEST UNDERSTAND THE WORDS *Christian*, *church*, and *denomination*. A *Christian* is who you are, a *church* is where you attend, and *denomination* represents the name of those in your circle of fellowship. As a Christian you visualize a specific group that believes alike, when visualizing the church you see a building, and when picturing a denomination you see bishops and overseers who believe alike. However, there are some important facts you should know about these three words.

First, neither Christ Himself nor His original chosen apostles ever called themselves *Christians* in the four Gospels. They were known as *disciples*, a word used 243 times in 231 verses in the New Testament. The Greek word *disciples* is *mathetes*, and refers to someone who learns under a teacher; someone who is a pupil. The word *Christian* is used twice (Acts 26:28; 1 Pet. 4:16), and *Christians* (plural) once in Acts 11:26—a total of three times. The Greek word *Christian* is *Christianos*, meaning *a follower of Christ*. However, the emphasis is on who His followers were and if they were and are His disciples.

Second is the word *church*. In the four Gospels Christ referred to the *church* three times in two verses, all in Matthew's Gospel (Matt. 16:18; 18:17). A theological definition of the church is an institution established by Christ for those who sustain a relationship with Him. The Greek word *church* is *ekklesia*, coming from two words *ek*, meaning, "out of," and *kaleo*, meaning, "call." It can mean "to call out of"—out of sin, out of the world's way of thinking. The word was not a new word but was used among the Greeks in the time of Christ.

The *ekklesia* was a political term for an assembly of Greek citizens, who would be assembled together in the town's square by the blasting of a trumpet. It was these citizens who held the ultimate power (including voting power) over any form of government that arose. In the city of Athens, Greece, they were summoned by law four times in thirty-six or thirty-seven days, or about forty times each year. It was this organized group that voted in the laws, the leaders, and made the political decisions of the city in the Greek state. If a Greek government became corrupt, it was the responsibility of the majority of the *ekklesia* to reject them, collapse the government, and set forth a new one within one day. It is interesting that Jesus used this word to identify His new organization, which we call *the church*. However, Christ used the word *church* only three times in the Gospels, but He referred to this *ekklesia* as a *kingdom*!

The word *kingdom* is used in the four Gospels 127 times, and 157 times in 150 verses in the New Testament. The Greek word *kingdom* is the same in all references, *basileia*, which is not just a kingdom with human subjects but a royal kingdom headed by a king. Christ used the phrases "kingdom of God" and "kingdom of heaven" when referring to His organized body on earth and to the family of God in heaven.

Your Position in the Kingdom

In the earlier days of all full-gospel churches, the emphasis of the ministers, pastors, teachers, and evangelists was placed upon the denomination first, the local church second, and the phrase "kingdom of God" was seldom if ever mentioned. It was expected that once you *joined the church* as a member, you were to remain loyal and unwaveringly faithful to the denomination, its leadership, and its various outreaches. For example, when I received denominational license to preach at age eighteen, I was informed by state leaders that they expected me to preach only in the churches within my denomination, as by preaching in other groups I would be *working against the church* (as though the other groups were not a part of the "real church"). This mind-set was as hard as a cement sidewalk in the minds of all state and national leaders. At age eighteen I walked into a state evangelism director's office of the denomination and began to tell him about two Methodist women who received the gift of the Holy Spirit in a revival in Davis, West Virginia. His response was, "Did they leave the Methodist church and join the local church?"

I responded, "No. They went back to help other church members understand the Holy Spirit." Without cracking a smile, he leaned over his desk and said, "I doubt their experience unless they come our way and join the church." I walked out that day and realized I was cut out of a different cookie cutter than these guys. After ministering in other denominations, Charismatic churches, and non-denominational churches, I was tagged as, "A young man who just doesn't work with the system." I reminded them, "I am not in man's system, but I am in the kingdom!" Every action I began to take was geared to building up the kingdom of God in the local churches, ignoring the specific denominational tag they may have.

Since we are in a kingdom that operates from kingdom principles and will, in the future, be ruled by the King of kings (Rev. 19:16), you must understand your present position. The world calls us *Christians*, but God's Word calls you, "Sons and daughters!" There were women Christ healed that He addressed as "Daughter" (Matt. 9:22; Mark 5:34) and on one occasion in a synagogue He addressed a woman as a "daughter of Abraham" (Luke 13:16). Christ also healed men and called them "son" (Matt. 9:2). In the last days God promises to pour out His Spirit upon "sons and daughters" (Joel 2:28–29). Those who receive Christ's redemptive covenant are given power to "become children of God" (John 1:12). Those led by the Spirit of God are the sons of God (Rom. 8:14). John said we are now the children of God, but it is yet to be seen what we shall be (1 John 3:2). I love the name *Christian*, but believers must see themselves as more than Christians who attends a church. We are in a royal family and are adopted into the covenant as a son or a daughter, giving us special rights, privileges, and levels of authority.

Our problem in Western Christianity is we have been so accustomed to titles, church names, and denominational tags that when we meet other believers, instead of seeing the big picture of the kingdom of God, we begin tagging them: "Oh they are Baptists. Those are charismatics. They attend a Pentecostal church." There is little understanding about the kingdom, what it is, how it operates, and the authority it releases. For example, when I say, "the United States," you may picture a giant map with forty-eight states then Alaska and Hawaii—a total of fifty. However, if I say, "the state of Alabama or Tennessee," you don't picture an entire map, but one state out of fifty. Alabama is not *the* United States as there must be a unit of fifty states to officially be the United States. However Alabama is part of the United States.

When I say "kingdom of God," it includes all born-again Baptists, Methodists, Pentecostals, charismatics, and other groups of denominations (notice the word *nations* in *denominations*). However, those denominations have thousands of individual churches that make up their particular *nation*. The challenge has been to merge each individual state (church nation) forming one nation called the *kingdom of God*. Since each group hangs around their own group, defending their own personal interpretation of Scripture, we must discover our individual position and authority in our own life, or rediscover our kingdom of authority.

Dominion and Authority Over "Creeps" and "People"

At the beginning of Creation, God gave mankind dominion over things on earth. We read:

> And God blessed them, and God said unto them, Be fruitful, and multiply, and replenish the earth, and subdue it: and have dominion over the fish of the sea, and over the fowl of the air, and over every living thing that moveth upon the earth.
>
> —Genesis 1:28, kjv

Twice in the Creation narrative God said that man would have *dominion* over the creation on earth (Gen. 1:26, 28). The Hebrew word *dominion* is *radah*, and it has numerous meanings, including "bear rule over, to tread down, to crumble off and prevail against." Most ministers point out that man was given authority over the animal kingdom, based on these two verses. Man certainly has this dominion as he can hunt any animal, and even train a giant elephant and tame a dangerous lion for a circus. However, notice man's dominion is also over "every *creeping* thing" (v. 26) and "every *living* thing" (v. 28). This phrase "living thing" is used eight times in the Old Testament (Gen. 1:28; 6:19; 8:1, 17; Lev. 11:10; 20:25; Job 12:10; Ps. 145:16). In the context of these scriptures the phrase alludes to animals, birds, fish, and creatures that crawl or walk on the ground. Job, however, says, "In whose hand is the life of every living thing, and the breath of all mankind?" (Job 12:10). When Adam was formed, God breathed into his nose, and Adam became a "living being" (Gen. 2:7). God gave man dominion over every living thing, which would include not only the animal kingdom but also those living beings that come forth from our loins—our children! This is why powerful intercession works—because the prayer warrior is exercising dominion that was given to mankind from the beginning of Creation.

The word *creeping* in Hebrew is *remes*, and generally refers to reptiles that crawl on the ground. This is the general meaning throughout the Old Testament where this word is used twenty-six times in twenty-six verses. Satan used a *serpent* in the garden to beguile Eve, resulting in the serpent being cursed to crawl on its belly (Gen. 3:14). The king of the reptilian kingdom is the serpent, as snakes are the most disliked and the venomous ones the most dangerous of all reptiles. Man's dominion is also over the "creeping things." One meaning of *dominion* is to tread or trample upon, reminding me of the words of Jesus:

> Behold, I give you the authority to trample on serpents and scorpions, and over all the power of the enemy, and nothing shall by any means hurt you.
> —LUKE 10:19

The power and influence of the serpent belongs under our feet, as Paul wrote:

> And the God of peace will crush Satan under your feet
> shortly.
> —ROMANS 16:20

God's covenant family has dominion over the creeping things—
both in the natural and spiritual realm. I am reminded that in
the human realm there are at times some rather *creepy* people. I
recall during one of our prayer times at the OCI ministry, one
of our young single women came to me and Pastor Mark saying,
"That man is following me around, and he is giving me the *creeps*."
Neither me nor Mark will permit any of our young women of God
or smaller children to be stalked by some creepy person, and we
will take dominion over their sneaking around.

The Old Testament uses the word *dominion*, while the New
Testament used the word *authority*. Man's original dominion
at Creation was over the natural world, but the New Testament
authority is over the spirit world. This word is used thirty-five
times in thirty-two verses. The common Greek word for *authority*
is *exousia*, and refers to a level of authority that is legally given
from a higher power to a lesser power from a judicial sense. I would
compare it to giving a family member the power of attorney to sign
legal papers on behalf of another. The signature in a court of law is
equal to the person it represents and will stand up in any court case,
if done legally and properly.

The spiritual authority behind the Word of God and the name
of Jesus becomes the two weapons of war in any spiritual battle. At
the name of Jesus every knee will bow, "things" in heaven, in earth,
and under the earth (Phil. 2:10, KJV).

Citizens in the Kingdom

As long as a believer believes that he or she is only a church member,
forgiven of sins, and on the way to heaven, that person will never

tap into the benefits of the kingdom. There are two opposing king-doms working on earth: the kingdom of Satan and the kingdom of God (Matt. 12:26–28). Satan's kingdom is controlled by darkness, but God's is dominated by light. In the beginning God created night and day, darkness and light (Matt. 6:23; 1 Thess. 5:5). When I say "light and darkness," many will picture nighttime and sun-light or daytime. However, when speaking of spiritual darkness and light, these words can be metaphors. Darkness can allude to spiri-tual ignorance and light to spiritual knowledge.

When a person has been ignorant of truth and suddenly comes to the knowledge of truth, we say that person "saw the light." Peter spoke of God calling us out of darkness into God's marvelous light (1 Pet. 2:9). People remain in bondage because they remain in igno-rance. The assignment of the kingdom is to call people to repent because the kingdom is at hand. Our second assignment is to understand that we are living in a visible world serving an invisible God who manifested an invisible kingdom through Christ, making the kingdom available to believers on earth. God's intent was to have "one Lord, one faith, one baptism" (Eph. 4:5) or one unified kingdom. However, after the death of the apostles and the rise of heretical teachers from the first through the fourth centuries, the church became divided.

When we know who we really are and our position, along with how God views His kingdom, our worship, prayer life, and daily activity will change. The New Testament uses different words when it comes to the kingdom versus the church. The inspired New Testament uses these words: *sons and daughters* (Acts 2:17; 2 Cor. 6:18), *citizens* (Eph. 2:19), and *ambassadors* (2 Cor. 5:20); all three of which make up a kingdom. When a king has sons and daughters, it makes them heirs of the kingdom. Paul said if we were God's chil-dren then we were "heirs of God and joint heirs with Christ" (Rom.

8:17). The Greek word *citizens* used in Luke is the word *polites*, from which we get the word *politics*. As a citizen, we are leaders in a future kingdom government. Christ will return with the saints to set up a kingdom in Jerusalem for a thousand years (Rev. 20:4), placing the control of all world governments upon His shoulders (Isa. 9:6–7).

The word *ambassadors* refers to an older leader who serves as a representative for a nation. The body of Christ (the church) is called by Peter "a chosen generation, a royal priesthood, a holy nation" (1 Pet. 2:9). The idea of believers being ambassadors is significant, since the kingdom is both heavenly (kingdom of heaven) and earthly (kingdom of God working on earth). America builds expensive and elaborate embassies throughout the world, often in third world poverty-stricken countries. If an American is visiting a foreign nation, has a valid passport, and gets into difficulties or danger, that American can find his way to the US embassy. The moment he steps foot past the huge iron gates onto the embassy property, it is as though he is in the United States, and he is provided the full protection of the US government. Ambassadors on a compound are not under the same economic difficulties that the nation they dwell in may be having. When a third world country is short on food, the ambassadors have food shipped in. If the currency collapses, they will operate in the currency of America. If they are taken hostage, (under most administrations) the military is called in to protect the compound or get the ambassadors out.

The parallels are amazing. As ambassadors we are citizens living in a country that is not our actual home, as heaven is our final destination. We are "not of this world" (world system). The local church becomes our embassy and has a powerful promise that the "gates of hell will not prevail against it" (Matt. 16:18). Our passport giving us access to and from one nation to another is the Great

Commission to "go into all the world and preach the gospel" (Mark 16:15). The economic promises of blessing and prosperity found in the laws of the kingdom are not contingent upon the economic shaking in the world's kingdoms. There is also diplomatic immunity for ambassadors when crossing borders, as they can carry sensitive information in a diplomatic pouch with a seal that cannot be opened or searched. There is a special prayer language given by the Holy Spirit to each son and daughter, citizen, and ambassador that is a communication line between Christ and the believer that cannot be tapped into or interrupted by any outside kingdom.

When we quit thinking traditional *church* and instead think *kingdom*, then when sickness, trouble, or sudden disaster arises we won't be searching out the pastor to come and hopefully get an emergency prayer through to God, or depending upon some saint we believe is closer to God than us who will touch God for us. We will open our mouths and begin to pray, decree, and prophesy, as spiritual authority is not just for preachers, but also for all citizens in the kingdom.

The first Adam was given dominion over "living things," but the last Adam, Christ, has given us dominion to make dead things live again. When a person is in total ignorance and blinded by the god of this world, he or she dwells in the land of the shadow of death. Spiritual revelation, illumination, and light will pierce the veil of ignorance and release the knowledge of God, illuminating the dark places.

In the New Testament believers are promised both power (Acts 1:8) and authority (Luke 10:19). The power promised to believers when we receive the Holy Spirit is transferrable through prayer and the laying on of hands (Acts 6:6; 8:18; 13:3; 1 Tim. 4:14). Authority, however, is released through your words. Christ preached with such authority that Roman soldiers said, "No man ever spoke like this

Man" (John 7:46). Eyewitnesses of His ministry commented, "For with authority He commands even the unclean spirits, and they obey Him" (Mark 1:27).

I have heard thousands of messages from hundreds of ministers since I was a child. Many messages and services I have long forgotten, but the ones that stand out are those that were preached not just with informative content, but also with such authority that people would stand to their feet before the word was completed. This same type of authority can be released through prayer, when you understand you are a member of the greatest kingdom in the universe and have been given authority over all of the powers of the enemy!

CHAPTER 12

PAUL and ESTHER— PREPARATION for DESTINY

W HEN BIBLICALLY INFORMED NATIONS CLASH WITH culture, and the righteous are in danger of extinction while evil men rise like smoke from a pit, God will raise up a voice of authority to close the pit, clear the smoke, and clarify the truth. One statement spoken to Esther by her uncle sums up this principle of God selecting a person to reverse the trends and save a nation:

> For if you remain completely silent at this time, relief and deliverance will arise for the Jews from another place, but you and your father's house will perish. Yet who knows whether you have come to the kingdom for such a time as this?
>
> —ESTHER 4:14

Some people dream of living at another time in history. Consider living in the original Garden of Eden. Life was like a fantasy until sin stained paradise. Imagine leaving a self-watered lush garden growing with every form of fruit and plant life, and being banished to a cursed earth where dirt and sweat were your new twin companions. Later the first couple deals with a duel over an offering in which a jealous son slew an innocent brother. Up to that point no one had ever died on the planet.

What about the days of Noah and the incredible ark he built? Sounds like an interesting construction job until you realize the reason this preacher became a lone contractor for God: the earth was corrupt and filled with violence, while giant men tormented people and scoffers mocked a man and his three sons for building a future floating zoo.

Perhaps it would have been more exciting to travel alongside Abraham when God revealed Himself and His covenant. Your journey with God's man of faith would have included famines, wars with five kings, and the burning destruction of four major cities.

As a teenage minister I felt cheated that I was not born at the time of the great tent revivals where overflow crowds poured in hungry for God's presence. That was until I realized that air-conditioning, padded seats, carpet, and restaurants to eat in were more advantageous than hot tents, metal folding chairs, sawdust, and few restaurants to fellowship in after the service.

As God prepares you for your future assignments, He often will use both the good and bad experiences of your life as part of your training, preparing your character and faith. Saul of Tarsus is a prime example. Saul was a Pharisee who trained under a noted rabbi named Gamaliel, and was himself being trained to be a chief rabbi in Jerusalem. Seeing the Christian faith emerging in Jerusalem, Saul considered the multitudes to be following a new cult that threatened the ancient traditions of the Jewish fathers, challenging portions of the Law. In his zeal Saul persecuted believers from city to city, arresting leaders and providing legal papers for their arrests and deaths. Saul was a champion defender of the laws and traditions of the Jews. On his way to Damascus to arrest Christians, he was interrupted by Christ who blinded his eyes, spoke to his mind, and changed his heart.

Saul of Tarsus, the religious zealot, became Paul the apostle, the Christian. He was not considered one of the original twelve apostles, but he informed readers that after Christ appeared to Peter, the twelve, the five hundred, and to James, He then appeared to him (see Acts 9). Paul wrote an interesting observation about himself in 1 Corinthians 15:8–9:

> Then last of all He was seen by me also, as by one born out of due time. For I am the least of the apostles, who am not worthy to be called an apostle, because I persecuted the church of God.

The phrase "born out of due time" is a Greek phrase referring to a woman having a *miscarriage* or an untimely birth. Paul was an unbeliever at the time Christ was ministering on earth, training His apostles and pouring into them His life-changing revelation. Paul felt like an immature and weak child born out of his season, and he felt unworthy to be called an apostle. One unusual way of viewing Paul's conversion is that just as with the Levites there were thirteen individual tribal leaders forming thirteen tribes in Israel, so with Matthias replacing Judas, and Paul's seeing Christ (a requirement to be an apostle), Paul could be ranked as the thirteenth apostle.

Look at Saul's conversion from God's perspective. When the church was birthed, three thousand Jews were converted, and in a second wave of conversions five thousand more were later added to the church (Acts 4:4). There were no Gentile converts until Acts

10. Paul's conversion was recorded in Acts 9, prior to the Gentile's grafting into the covenant. After his conversion, Paul spent about three years in Arabia in prayer, receiving the revelation of Christ (Gal. 1:17–18). God needed a wise, knowledgeable teacher for the new Gentiles entering the church, and thus Paul fit the description. He had been on the other side of the fence, knew the Law, and was now a teacher of grace. It was Paul's training, background, and knowledge that marked him as a chosen vessel, as God used each aspect of his past as gifts to speak, write, and lead the church.

I often wondered if there was a *trigger* that propelled Saul toward his conversion. I believe it was the *seed prayer* of Stephen that released Saul's soul to his destiny. Saul agreed to Stephen's death, holding the coats of Stephen's rock-throwing mob, yet in his final moments Stephen cried out, "Lord, do not charge them with this sin" (Acts 7:60). Stephen publicly cried out that he saw Jesus standing at the right hand of God (v. 56). It was shortly thereafter that Saul was converted. The blood of Stephen, the first Christian martyr, became the scarlet thread reaching from the window of heaven to the heart of this Pharisee, pulling him into the kingdom.

God Prepares Your Destiny Through Life Events

When I made a pilgrimage to Israel in 1985, what I saw stirred a prophetic fire within me. Returning home, I began writing a small feature prophetic update in our two-color 8-by-12-inch page *Voice of Evangelism* publication, sent to about thirty-five hundred people. After several years I commented to my wife, "I don't know why I am interested in prophecy and take the time for all of this research. I think it might be a waste of energy." However, I continued researching, writing, and presenting prophetic updates each Saturday night during our revivals. I had no concept that God had placed this desire to understand the signs of the times and end-time events in my spirit to prepare me for a worldwide television program that would be aired in 249 nations. In 1985 in Israel I had no clue that in fifteen years, *Manna-Fest* would air up to six months of its programs taped in Israel, with about half of the programs emphasizing prophetic insights. The *desire* God had placed in my heart was actually His *preparation* for His will to be done, in His time.

In the mid and late 1980s I had no clue what was coming to the world—the breakup of the Iron Curtain of Communism in Eastern Europe and in the Soviet Union, the return of Jews from the Gentile nations, the Oslo peace plan, the Gulf War parts one and two, and the shocking terror attack on 9/11. These and other stunning events left people wondering how they fit into ancient biblical predictions concerning the time of the end and how it would impact them personally.

It would be many years *after* we began our weekly tele-cast, *Manna-Fest*, that I remembered a prayer I had prayed as a sixteen-year-old just feeling the call into the ministry and having an unquenchable thirst for the knowledge of God. I recall being in fervent prayer and petitioning the Lord to allow me to have the same spirit of understanding as Daniel, the apocalyptic prophet from Babylon, gifted to understand the meaning of mysterious dreams and visions. It was my desire to know God, not just from what I had been taught from a child, but to learn those things of which I had no knowledge, gaining understanding into God's deeper mysteries. God did hear that young skinny boy pray, and today the results of the prayer are evident.

We think that God only uses the *positive elements* of our lives in His purpose, but often the early battles and struggles become the fuel for the fire of purpose and serve as a part of our testimony that reaches others. Esther was a perfect example. She had lost both of her parents as a young girl, and was being raised by her near relative, Mordecai. She was living as an exile outside of her native Israel in Persia, a nation whose strict laws were their strength, but still they allowed idols and false gods to be worshipped. She was also Jewish, which at that time would have worked against her aspiration to be queen—if those selecting her in the beauty contest would have known. Esther had a lot working against her but also a lot working for her—mainly her *confidence* in God! It was her stunning *beauty* that caught the king's attention. Winning this beauty contest when aligned with the best-looking young women in one hundred twenty-seven provinces was no small task. However, her rise to prominence was actually a *divine setup* for her to have a position of royal authority in order to save the Jews in the Persian provinces.

Esther's story holds numerous important applications. First is that God will conceal you from others to guard your future. Dating the wrong person can lead to a wrong marriage. Working in the wrong place can lead to wrong relationships. Esther was concealed from the king and surrounded by guards and virgin women until the right moment. The second application Esther teaches us involves risk. It was against Persian laws for the queen to approach the king without the king calling upon her first. There was already a bitter taste in the king's administration because of the lack of protocol from the former queen, whom the king had expelled from her position and the kingdom. Esther could literally be expelled from the palace and stripped of her position, and the king could demand a divorce. She had to risk everything, for if she remained silent her people would die. She determined, "If I perish, I perish" (Esther 4:16). Our what-ifs are risk stealers. These what-if stealers generate fear of a possible bad outcome, thus we would rather do nothing, leaving things as status quo rather than attempt something and fail. Speaking of risk, never play games with your eternal soul or risk an early death by putting dangerous substances in your body. There are, however, times you must step out of the boat to walk on water or dip in water for a healing. The difficulty of the task is only in your eyes and not in God's, as with God nothing shall be impossible (Luke 1:37).

I knew a family whose son was struggling with alcohol. He would drink in the house in his room, but never went out to a bar joining with others. The dad was frustrated and disheartened, when a minister told him, "You know we both teach against drinking alcohol. However, your son will not go out to bars and neither does he drink and drive. We need to believe that despite his actions, the Lord is protecting him by keeping him in the house and guarding him from an accident, a DWI, or other form of disaster. Let's pray for protection until he is delivered." When you have difficulty meeting or making new friends, it may be that the Lord is guarding you to preserve your destiny.

Another great principle is how God uses what you have to create what you need. Moses held a rod, which became a miracle stick; David used a slingshot and stones, which decked a giant. Shamgar's choice was an ox goad; Gideon blew trumpets; and Samson picked up a jawbone to defeat Israel's enemies. Two widows in the Bible found something in their houses that God used to multiply a blessing to meet their financial and personal needs (1 Kings 17:9–16; 2 Kings 4:1–7). Esther had no wealth, Persian education, or family lineage that would impress the king, but she had beauty and poise. The king had one hundred twenty-seven individual virgin women to choose from, and Esther took the contest hands down. If you are creative, funny, a social butterfly, or an outgoing personality who loves meeting people, these are your creative gifts that God uses to exalt you in your workplace and position.

I have learned not to despise seasonal battles as those battles are what seasons you, just like the spices in a chef's favorite dish. Every generation has its battles, from persecution and false teachings, to alcohol and drug addictions, to fainting and desiring to quit. Every generation has its knockdowns from which they need to get back up. Samson was down and had to get back up. David fell, yet he got back up. Noah didn't stay drunk in his tent, but he had to recoup and get back into living out his final days. Peter had to repent and pick himself up and get back on the Gospel trail and feed the sheep.

It is God Himself who positions each person at the right place at the right time—even with the right circumstances. What if the righteous men and women who had a specific assignment had forsaken their callings or resisted to follow through in God's ordained process? What if Esther had feared approaching the king, or if Joseph had gone to prison, become discouraged, and lost sight of his dreams? What if Simon Peter had allowed his failure to overwhelm his faith, leaving the ministry and never standing at Pentecost leading three thousand Jews to Christ?

Preparation for your future must be personal and at times done in private. It required Esther to prepare for twelve months for the king's beauty contest. Her preparation included "purification" and "oil of myrrh...sweet spices and perfumes" (Esther 2:9–12, AMP). A clean heart and a clear conscience are the power lines connecting God's favor, voice, and power with the spirit and mind of the receiver. Purification comes in two methods: purification of the human spirit and soul by applying the blood of Christ, purging our sins, and washing our conscience (Heb. 9:14); and through cleaning ourselves from filthiness of the flesh and spirit by laying aside the weight and sins that slow us down (Heb. 12:1–2). Self-purification is when we use our willpower and choose to remove from us any spiritual hindrances that are appealing to our flesh and detrimental to our spirit; such could be habits, chemical substances, pornography, and items that plant bad seeds that produce weeds. Purification always preceded power, and power releases the presence of the King, Jesus Christ.

Esther's appearance and physical body were prepared with numerous oils. This was to make her skin soft and glowing, increasing her appearance and beauty. In the Torah oil was a sacred substance poured over the head of the prophet, priests, and kings to anoint them for service. When the oil was applied, the Holy Spirit would then come upon the person as evidence of his high calling (1 Sam. 10:1; 1 Sam. 16:13). The oil always symbolizes the presence and anointing of the Holy Spirit. The unction and anointing of the Holy Spirit is imparted when a believer is baptized in the Holy Spirit, as we receive power after the Holy Spirit comes upon us (Acts 1:8). However, learning to operate in the numerous types of anointing and being sensitive to the Holy Spirit requires time and experience. Just as Esther was covered in oil in private before being placed on public display, we must be filled and refilled with the Spirit in private prayer and devotion before our gifts or ministry are placed on public display.

All struggles—body, soul, or spirit—preventing a person from receiving Christ's redemptive covenant are always about the *future* and not the *present*. It is difficult to understand why one child, one companion, or one relative will struggle more than the others. If you pay careful attention, each of these individuals has one specific gifting that, if tapped into by the Holy Spirit, can become a tool of evangelism, a weapon of war against Satan, a testimony to win others, or a gift to draw people to them.

When I was a teenage minister in Virginia, one of my spiritual mentors was Bishop Marion H. Kennedy, the state bishop for our denomination in Virginia. MH was from Tupelo, Mississippi, and when growing up, his family lived near and was good friends with Vernon Presley, the father of Elvis Presley. Marion's parents bought Elvis's brother his first guitar. In fact, when Vernon died, Marion Kennedy was contacted to perform the funeral services. Bishop Kennedy related to me that the Presley family attended a Pentecostal church, and Elvis began singing at a young age. However, when Elvis was older, he desired to sing for a gospel group, tried out, and was turned down, basically because they didn't feel he could sing well enough. The rest is history. Elvis did at times sing gospel, and was greatly touched by gospel music. However, what if his gift would have been used to reach youth for Christ in concerts, similar to the contemporary gospel groups today? Imagine the influence the man and gift held, which no doubt was originally intended for use in the kingdom.[1]

Choosing Less but Gaining More

In the mid 1980s Pam and I met a man who served as one of Elvis's backup singers. In a church in Tennessee he shared his personal testimony of how he was raised in a strict full-gospel minister's home, had strayed away, but came back to Christ. He went to Elvis to inform him that he would be leaving the group and how Christ had restored him back to his faith. He said Elvis told him about his own upbringing and how he had a love for God. He also said that he wished he could make a break and do the same thing, but he had too many contracts and too many people depending upon him for their income.[2] Elvis died on August 16, 1977, at age 42. His next concert—that he never made it to—was in my hometown area in Roanoke, Virginia. Today he still sells more records than any other singer or musician. Had he gone ahead and returned to his roots, he would have continued to have great success. I have "inside information" from a friend close to the Presley family that told me Elvis knew he was going to die soon and had made his heart ready to meet God.[3]

At times I see young Hollywood stars in the music industry that have millions of dollars to "blow" and spend their huge sums on mansions, elite vacations, huge planes, diamonds, and glittering attractions, but they are leading millions of their followers down the wrong path. There are three in particular (I will not name them) who are noted in the secular music industry—who were all raised by Christian parents and yet they have chosen a life of fame and rejected the Christian values and instruction planted in them as a child. Without a divine intervention they will gain the whole world and at the end lose their souls (Matt. 16:26). Their gift was created from their mother's womb for the kingdom of God and their charisma to be a magnet, drawing large crowds to hear the name of Christ exalted in concerts across the nation. Instead of choosing the less popular "narrow" route and gaining eternity, they have chosen the wide road that leads to destruction (Matt. 7:13–14).

Moses was the adopted son of Pharaoh's daughter and his acceptance into the royal family provided him with the finest education, the most exquisite food and rooms in the greatest palace in the kingdom, with a potential to rise to a high position in the future. However, Moses was an Egyptian on the outside but a Hebrew on the inside. He chose to suffer (Heb. 11:25), was exiled because of a murder (Exod. 2:12–15), and lived in a barren desert wilderness for forty years. Moses chose the lesser life and eventually was given the greater responsibility. God used this prophet to bring millions of Jews out of bondage where he pastored them for forty years in a traveling tent revival. Just as God used Paul's education to teach the Gentiles faith in the Messiah, He also used Moses the shepherd to lead His flock, Israel, through a wilderness for forty years.

The "great things" you may think you are giving up are nothing compared to what you will gain when you seek first the kingdom of God and His righteousness (Matt. 6:33). Your obedience is the opportunity to walk through a door to your God-assigned destiny.

CHAPTER 13

BREAKING SATAN'S STRONGHOLDS ON YOUR BLOODLINE

T HE HEAVIEST BURDEN FOR A PARENT TO CARRY IS for his or her bloodline—his or her children and grand-children and their eternal destiny. Children are a heritage from the Lord and the greatest weight on a parent's heart. Adam and Eve lost their second son when their firstborn slew his brother in jealousy. The grandson of Noah, Canaan, was cursed by his grandfather for acts performed on Noah when he was drunk. Esau, in retaliation of his father blessing Jacob, married a heathen wife, who became a grief to his mother and father. Jacob's two sons, Simeon and Levi, slew an entire tribe because one of the men raped their sister. The prophet Samuel was a righteous man who heard God's voice at age twelve, but his own sons became immoral and corrupt. King David had one son who raped his half-sister, another son who attempted a coup, and a third who died in a civil uprising. Job's sons and daughters were tragically killed in a hurricane:

> While he was still speaking, another also came and said, "Your sons and daughters were eating and drinking wine in their oldest brother's house, and suddenly a great wind came from across the wilderness and struck the four corners of the house, and it fell on the young people, and they are dead; and I alone have escaped to tell you!" Then Job arose, tore his robe, and shaved his head; and he fell to the ground and worshiped.
>
> —JOB 1:18–20

I have met thousands of parents whose children were raised in a local church but today are spiritually AWOL. When questioning what they believe to be the *root cause* for their children's absence from God's house, there are common answers, including wrong influences, a private sin they enjoy yet avoiding any conviction of sin, and the devil hindering them. The *whys* are: "Why is my loved one not saved?" "Why do they have no concern for their spiritual destiny?" "Why are they not concerned about how their own children will turn out?"

There can actually be three often-undetected root causes why your family members avoid church.

Social Reasons

My father's generation was a Sunday go-to-meeting suit and tie generation, and no minister would have thought of preaching without a tie and jacket. The domination of denominational churches was replaced with independent churches, and the congregations became younger and the tendency was to dress more *business casual*. These churches grew fast, while the more traditional churches often just maintained their memberships. I recall a minister in a megachurch telling me that he read where 80 percent of the men in America do not own a suit. When inviting the average unchurched man to a church setting, many thought it required dressing up, and thus made numerous excuses for not showing up.

The Pentecostal-charismatic churches are noted for more *emotionally driven* worship. Often the pastor or a guest speaker will suggest for people to join hands in agreement in prayer. This is normal and easily accepted by members of these churches—but for a man who is not a believer to join hands with a stranger, especially another man, can be rather uncomfortable. This is not to say churches should avoid joining hands, but this can be an unspoken reason why some individuals, especially men, avoid churches.

I have met numerous men who don't enjoy carrying on a conversation with people they do not know. To them, going to a church means they will have to converse with different people, and they don't want to be asked questions and hear answers to questions they never asked. Many people, both men and women, are also apprehensive about attending a church, as perhaps years ago the members were known to be judgmental and opinionated when seeing how visitors dressed, the amount of makeup they wore, or the type of outward adornment (jewelry) they were wearing. These personal observations may seem insignificant to believers, but the adversary will use whatever hindrances and roadblocks available to build a stronghold in the minds of the unsaved.

Neurological Reasons

During my entire ministry I have never heard anyone explain the possibility that some don't attend church for neurological reasons. For example, when a person battles certain types of neurological challenges—bipolar disorder, types of autism and Asperger's syndrome—their view of their surroundings and of dealing with people can become a struggle. There are 1 to 1.5 million Americans living with an autism spectrum disorder, based on the autism prevalence rate of 1 in 110.[1] Asperger's syndrome is an autism spectrum disorder (ASD), and the Center for Disease Control has estimated that there are possibly 3.5 million people nationwide with ASD.[2]

Having personally dealt with a low-level spectrum of Asperger's myself, I totally understand the tension that a person encounters when being required to converse with a person or group of people with whom you are not familiar, perhaps having nothing in common. For those on the higher scale, being in a large crowd causes the jitters, and loud noises can actually hurt their ears. Individuals with this type of autism would prefer one or two friends instead of a group, sitting away from the crowd, and, at times, wear plugs in their ears, dulling outward sounds, when others see no need.

In one instance a young man's mother, to whom he was extremely close and dependent, passed away. The young man was unable to express any outward emotion such as crying. He also told me that it was virtually impossible for him to read another person's emotions and facial expressions. He could not discern if a person was pleased or displeased, even by that person's comments.

When a child or a loved one makes excuses for not attending church, we can assume it is because he or she is rebellious or totally uninterested. However, there may be neurological reasons that are not known or detected that can become a hindrance to the person becoming acquainted with godly people or a good community congregation of believers.

Economic Reasons

There is a perception outside the church that the church in general is simply a business that is after a person's money. Of course those with this perception never give an offering, pay tithes, or support any evangelistic or missionary project. Thus their complaining is an excuse to avoid attending any religious event, especially a local church. It should be pointed out, however, that when a family does experience economic challenges, they may be more apprehensive about attending church as they are concerned about paying for gas or whatever is required to go back and forth.

Spiritual Reasons

The ultimate reason for many avoiding a Christian gathering is spiritual reasons. First, according to John 12:40, the adversary has blinded the eyes and hardened the hearts of some, preventing them from receiving knowledge and being converted. Each human has two sets of eyes: one set that is natural and the other spiritual. It is possible to see but not understand what you are looking at, and it is possible to hear truth and be "dull of hearing," a phrase Paul used to describe his Hebrew readers (Heb. 5:11). The word *dull* means, "to be sluggish; not dull like a dull knife, but to have wax in your ears that blocks words from entering." Among others, their understanding is darkened (Eph. 4:18). There are numerous Greek words for *understanding* in the New Testament. Among those, one means an unintelligent person, or one lacking understanding (Matt. 15:16). Another refers to mentally putting facts together to form an understanding (Mark 12:33). In Luke 24:45 *understanding* refers to using your mind and intellect to make a decision. In 1 Corinthians 14:20, it refers to the need to stop thinking like children.

There can be numerous reasons why a person or a family refuses to be converted to Christ and to fellowship with a weekly gathering of believers. However, the ultimate reason for a lack of spiritual interest is summed up in one word: *unbelief.* It is impossible to receive any spiritual or, for that matter, physical and financial blessing or breakthrough if a person abides in unbelief.

One of the most remarkable stories of how unbelief grieves the heart of God was related to me by Mark Casto. Mark's paternal grandmother was a Christian, but she did not believe in the full-gospel message, including the manifestations of the Holy Spirit. When Mark's dad received the baptism in the Holy Spirit, his mother (Mark's grandmother) rebuked and criticized him. Eventually she ended up in a hospital in serious condition. On one occasion she saw a man appear before her bed. She asked him who he was, and he replied, "I am your guardian angel, and you have offended me!" This angelic messenger appeared to her twice, with the same message. She was in great fear, thinking he was a death angel and that she was going to die because God was displeased with her. When she asked, "What have I done?," the messenger said, "Because you do not believe in the supernatural you have offended me." The visitation removed the unbelief from her heart; she repented and became a member of the church!

The reason for understanding these often undetected excuses for a lack of interest in spiritual matters or attending church is to know how to identify the root cause preventing a sinner or backslider from serving Christ. When couples have marital difficulties or a person has addictions, a counselor often pulls back layers of surface junk to discover the root of the conflict.

I have suggested that if a person does not like dressing up, then let them attend church in a casual outfit or find a place where they can attend and not be considered out of place or judged for their outward appearance, since "man looks on the outward appearance, but the LORD looks at the heart" (1 Sam. 16:7). Should a person have difficulty with crowds, allow that person to sit in an area where he feels more secure and let him know there is no need to be a social butterfly—but just to come and enjoy the music and the Word. If a family is having financial difficulty, then offer to allow them to ride with you, or offer to bring their kids to church, even if the parents cannot or refuse to attend.

Growing up we would often blame the "old devil" for keeping people out of church. Yet in the ministry of Jesus individuals with evil spirits actually attended the synagogues on the Sabbath day. One of Christ first miracles, at Capernaum, was when a man controlled by an unclean spirit began crying out demanding Jesus to be quiet and leave them alone. Christ cast the spirit out causing quite a controversy among the quiet and refined attendees (Mark 1:20–27). On another occasion, on the Sabbath in a synagogue, Christ rebuked a spirit of infirmity and delivered a woman who was physically bound for eighteen years (Luke 13:10–16). The point is, individuals who are bound, oppressed and vexed by evil spirits do at times attend church. So it is not always the *devil* keeping them out. It is often the works of the flesh, the lack of desire, and at times pure laziness. Many are uninterested in being confronted with their sins and prefer to avoid a setting in which the presence of God confronts them as God did Adam, when God desired to know why Adam was hiding (Gen. 3:9). To avoid confronting their own personal demons, unconverted or backslidden individuals build their own mental reasoning to either excuse their sin, justify their weakness, or soothe their conscience. The adversary is very good at inspiring people to argue within themselves and come up with the "right" answers.

Wrong thinking creates strongholds. The Bible speaks of strongholds and how they must be "pulled down" (2 Cor. 10:4–5). The word *stronghold* was used by the Greeks when speaking of a castle or a military fortification that was built to prevent access. In Paul's writings strongholds are mental blocks or thinking that prevented spiritual breakthroughs. In the church setting it referred to false teachings contrary to the gospel and how the false teacher would figuratively seek a safe place or a shelter (stronghold) within the argument itself. The Greek word *stronghold* (*ochyroma*) was not used often in classical Greek, but the idea of pulling down a stronghold may be an allusion to the coasts of Paul's native Cilicia, where the rock fortresses were pulled down by the Romans on their attacks on Cilician pirates.

Just as the adversary will use a person's thinking, social reasoning, neurological reasoning, and economic difficulties to build up a mental stronghold, hindering them from going to the very place where their mental and spiritual chains can be broken, believers must also deal with wrong thinking and never allow human reasoning to exalt itself above the knowledge of God, but to pull down mental strongholds (2 Cor. 10:4–5).

When parents have asked me how they should pray for their prodigal son, daughter, or at times grandparents are concerned about their wayward grandchildren, I share how I pray for my own children. The first thing I do is thank God for giving me two wonderful children—a boy and a girl. I then declare that anyone who carries my DNA or my name (Stone) that is linked to my family, they will all be in the kingdom of God and not one will be missing. I ask God to protect them from harm, danger, and any disabling accident, and I assign a generational angel to be with them. At times when I have seen someone in my bloodline struggle and knew a demonic spirit was attacking them, my prayer became aggressive and a rebuking anointing began flowing through me as I rebuked the powers of the adversary, demanding them to "get their hands off" that person and for God to bring relief and restoration. It is also important to discover if there is a "root source" to their resistance to God—a hurt, an offense, a misunderstanding—that should be dealt with.

Parents should also pray in advance for the friends their children have, beginning at an early age, as many of their choices as teenagers will emerge out of peer pressure from those surrounding them. We have been blessed to homeschool both of our children and because their mother—my precious Pam—is intense as their instructor, their tests show they are advanced in knowledge above the public school systems nationally. My daughter hangs with a large group of homeschoolers, most are from Christian families, and this has served as a wonderful blessing in how she views social and moral issues. While not all parents can or even should homeschool, prayer for your child's friends and involvement in their lives is of upmost importance to their spiritual growth—at an early age.

Praying Until You Feel the Assurance

At times it takes very intense and consistent intercession to initiate a life-changing breakthrough in family members. Often when a parent or any believer engages in intense intercessory prayer coupled with a prayer burden, the seeker will receive an *assurance* before they see the actual *breakthrough*. The Greek word for *assurance* in the New Testament means *a complete and peaceful confidence in a matter* (1 Thess. 1:5; Heb. 6:11; 10:22). Once this inner assurance is received, it releases a calming effect that settles your mind or spirit, as God's still small voice prompts your perception that everything will be all right and you can move from *asking* God to *thanking* Him in advance. Isaiah wrote:

> The work of righteousness will be peace, and the effect of righteousness, quietness and assurance forever.
> —ISAIAH 32:17

When I was a teenage minister, I canned this feeling of assurance, "I know in my knower!" For example, there have been times I have prayed for individuals whose situations were so bleak that it required a supernatural intervention, or what we term a miracle to bring them back from the brink of death or destruction. However, when prayer was offered under the anointing of the Spirit, a peaceful calm erased the doubts and confusion. We left the hospital knowing that everything would be well.

Never cease to pray for your lost family members and begin thanking God when you sense an assurance. Remember, the peace of assurance will precede the actual breakthrough, often by days, weeks, and months. The best way to disrobe the assurance is in the words of Paul, when he wrote, "For we which have believed do enter into rest...." (Heb. 4:3, KJV). When faith and assurance collide, you will be at rest, even in the most severe storm...for even Christ could sleep through a storm *knowing* He was going over to the other side (Luke 8:22–25). God's assurance that He is and will be moving on your behalf will bring a mental, physical, and spiritual rest to you.

CHAPTER 14

RIZPAH–DEALING WITH THE **BIRDS** AND THE **BEASTS**

WHEN GROWING UP IN THE CHURCH I NEVER HEARD any minister speak about or give a sermon on the woman Rizpah. Yet her story is one of the most stirring and touching in the Bible, especially for parents who deeply love their children. The Scripture records godly men and women who saw their children suffer or die at an earlier age than they should. Job lost ten children in a wilderness windstorm when the house collapsed (Job 1:19). Lot had sons-in-law and daughters die in the fiery destruction of Sodom just after they mocked Lot's warning and refused to get out of Sodom before the judgment struck (Gen. 19:14). David lost an infant son through sickness, and other sons died who had rebelled against him and against God (2 Sam. 12:18; 2 Sam. 18:33).

This mother of Israel, Rizpah, lost her only two sons at the same time. Below is the biblical account:

But the king spared Mephibosheth the son of Jonathan, the son of Saul, because of the LORD's oath that was between them, between David and Jonathan the son of Saul. So the king took Armoni and Mephibosheth, the two sons of Rizpah the daughter of Aiah, whom she bore to Saul, and the five sons of Michal the daughter of Saul, whom she brought up for Adriel the son of Barzillai the Meholathite; and he delivered them into the hands of the Gibeonites, and they hanged them on the hill before the LORD. So they fell, all seven together, and were put to death in the days of harvest, in the first days, in the beginning of barley harvest.

Now Rizpah the daughter of Aiah took sackcloth and spread it for herself on the rock, from the beginning of harvest until the late rains poured on them from heaven. And she did not allow the birds of the air to rest on them by day nor the beasts of the field by night. And David was told what Rizpah the daughter of Aiah, the concubine of Saul, had done. Then David went and took the bones of Saul, and the bones of Jonathan his son, from the men of Jabesh Gilead who had stolen them from the street of Beth Shan, where the Philistines had hung them up, after the Philistines had struck down Saul in Gilboa.

—2 SAMUEL 21:7–12

The most difficult spiritual warfare is the type that continues for a longer, extended season, because long battles wear down even the most experienced soldiers. The most stressful level of conflict is when a parent must deal with the resistance or rebellion of sons or daughters. The parent is not only concerned with their lives on earth, but also with their final destination in eternity. The greatest struggle is dealing with rebellion in the bloodline.

Throughout the Scripture the clash between God and Satan has been over the "seed," the offspring of a man who is formed in the image and likeness of God (Gen. 1:26). Satan, the adversary, is threatened by an unknown future when a young man or woman catches on fire for God, for that godly young person can burn the chaff out of the lives of his or her friends through witnessing, teaching, and preaching the Word of God. Since the final generation prior to Christ's return is promised an outpouring of the Spirit, depths of Satan's hatred and anger will increase (Rev. 12:12). The promised outpouring of the Spirit on sons and daughters is the final prophecy to be fulfilled prior to the return of Christ (Joel 2:28–29; Acts 2:17–18).

Attacks at Harvest Times

At the timing of the death of Rizpah's two sons, it was *harvest time*. Throughout the Old Testament the harvest cycles were a great time of rejoicing in the fields, but also a time when the Hebrews must remain alert to the surprise attacks of the enemies. It was at the time of the barley harvest that the Jordan River flooded (Josh. 3:15), making it difficult for the children of Israel to transition from the past (the wilderness) to the future (the Promised Land). Metaphorically a flood can represent a sudden and unexpected storm that arises, making it difficult to transition from one place to another. At times the enemy comes against us like a flood (Isa. 59:19). It was at the time of the wheat harvest that the Philistines burnt alive with fire the wife of Samson and her father (Judg. 15:1–6). The men at Beth Shemesh became careless during the wheat harvest when removing the mercy seat (lid) from the ark of the covenant, costing the lives of fifty thousand and seventy men (1 Sam. 6:13–19). In the New Testament the harvest is the time when souls are ripe to receive the message of the kingdom, and the harvest is the "end of the age" (Matt. 13:39). It is at the time of the end-time harvest (prior to Christ's return) that the most intensive battles will rage.

In ancient Israel the barley and wheat were stacked in piles and had to be protected until they were gathered in jars and sealed with the owner's seal, then stored in barns and other safe chambers. This is the reason that Boaz was sleeping at night near the piles of his grain. There had been a severe famine for ten years in the region, and many nomadic tribes would have loved to invade Bethlehem and take these grain piles from Boaz back to their own cities. Boaz knew that it required additional caution during certain seasons to guard the precious seed (Ruth 3:7). Do not be surprised at the attacks that will come against your "seed"—your bloodline and family—in these last days, as the enemy is not just after your "harvest," he is also after your "seed," or your sons and daughters. This is because your seed has a dynamic promise of the Spirit being poured out upon them in the last days (Joel 2:28–29). The adversary despises the time of harvest because it is the fruit of your travailing prayers and unmovable faith.

The Zeal of Rizpah

Rizpah was the daughter of Aiah and a concubine of the former king of Israel, Saul. This narrative about Rizpah, who stood in the gap for five months, reveals numerous practical and spiritual principles required to be followed by a true intercessor in order to obtain spiritual results. The name *Rizpah* comes from the Hebrew root word *rasap*. The verb means, "to fit together" (used in Song of Sol. 3:10). Other derivatives are *rispa*, meaning, "pavement." What is called the unused root letter (*rsp*) bears out the feminine noun, *rispa*, meaning, "a hot coal or stone." The word is used in two instances: when Elijah was hungry and the angel prepared the prophet a meal on a hot stone (1 Kings 19:6), and when Isaiah saw the Lord high and lifted up and a seraphim placed hot coals on his lips (Isa. 6:6). The *hot stones* in Hebrew use the root letters for the name *Rizpah*.[1] When reading of the actions of Rizpah, it is understandable why her name in Hebrew means "glowing or hot coal." There was a burning desire in her heart that could not be quenched. James reminds believers that the "effective, fervent prayer of a righteous man avails much" (James 5:16). This is a prayer offered with energy and determination.

During the days of Saul, he had slain men among the Gibeonites, a tribal clan with whom Joshua had entered a covenant of peace (Josh. 11:19). Breaking the law of shedding innocent blood, God's justice demanded that judgment come upon Israel in the form of a three-year severe famine. It was David who discovered the reason behind the lack of rain and God's punishment as he sought God to reverse the curse on the land. In the days of the law it was an "eye for eye, tooth for tooth" (Exod. 21:24), and blood for blood. It was Saul who had slain the Gibeonites, thus the Gibeonites required the death of Saul's sons (of his bloodline) to stop the divine retribution of the famine. There were a total of seven sons: five from Merab and two from Rizpah, who were given over to the hands of the Gibeonites and hung on the wall of the city (2 Sam. 21:8–9).

Rizpah lost her two sons, Armoni and Mephiboseth, while Merab lost five sons (2 Sam. 21:8). The only oddity of this fact is there is no biblical record of the response of Merab when her sons were slain and hung on the wall. Merab is not on the rock with Rizpah, and she seems to have disappeared from the scene. These two responses illustrate the responses of mothers today: those who go into intercession when horrible circumstances strike their bloodline, and the other mothers who may be grieving and filled with pain, but accept the events as they are, continuing on with their lives.

Some spiritual breakthroughs only come by a combination of prayer and fasting. Prayer reveals your desire to God, but fasting reveals your determination for the answer from God. Rizpah is a wonderful picture of a woman intercessor who refuses to give up until she sees her two sons removed from the wall of the city, a place of public humiliation. Rizpah took sackcloth and spread it on the ground. In the West we picture sackcloth as a burlap bag with arm holes cut in the left and right top corners. Sackcloth in the ancient days was actually a sack made of black goat's hair, used for holding grain, and was worn in times of national or personal mourning. The black or dark color has always been a sign of mourning or great grief. It is common at a funeral for the men, and often the women, to wear black or a dark color, and grief and sorrow are represented as dark seasons in the lives of surviving family members. It was also common during national mourning or repentance to throw *ashes* (these were from burned wood) upon one's head as a sign of humility. Jacob rent his clothes and put sackcloth around his waist (Gen. 37:34). When mourning over the death of his son Abner, David tore his clothes and placed sackcloth over his body (2 Sam. 3:31). Mordecai, the uncle of Esther, also tore his clothes, putting on sackcloth and ashes (Esther 4:1).

The first principle in intercession is understanding the power of humility and the blessing which follows.

> And whoever exalts himself will be humbled, and he who humbles himself will be exalted.
> —MATTHEW 23:12

> God resists the proud, but gives grace to the humble.
> —JAMES 4:6

> Humble yourselves in the sight of the Lord, and He will lift you up.
> —JAMES 4:10

Humble yourselves under the mighty hand of God, that He
may exalt you.

—1 PETER 5:6

Rizpah spread the sackcloth on the "rock." During harvest times,
the barley and wheat were laid out on a round natural rock called
a *threshing floor*. The barley or wheat grain on the threshing floor
rock was rolled over and crushed by a threshing instrument (2 Sam.
24:22) made of wood and set with sharp stones or pieces of iron to
separate the grain from the outer shells and stalks that made up the
chaff, which was later gathered and burned in a fire (Matt. 3:12).[2]
Rizpah knew that this rock was where the next harvest of grain
would be brought, thus she would remain on the rock until she
gained the attention of the king.

The lyrics of a hymn, "Rock of Ages, cleft for me, let me hide
myself in Thee," illustrate the Old Testament metaphor of *rock*
to symbolize the stability and strength of God.[3] "I proclaim the
name of the LORD…He is the Rock" (Deut. 32:3–4). "The LORD
is my rock and my fortress" (2 Sam. 22:2). "Who is a rock, except
our God?" (2 Sam. 22:32). Rizpah stayed on this rock during the
heat and the cold, the sunshine and the clouds, the new moon of
darkness and under the glow of the full moon. Staying on the rock
represents remaining in consistent intercession without being distracted by surrounding circumstances.

The Birds and the Beasts

One revealing part of this story is Rizpah's determination to drive
off the birds and the beasts. This grieving mother was living on
the rock near the bodies of her two sons. The Gibeonites kept the
bodies of these seven men on the wall of the city. Rizpah drove
away the *birds* in the day and the wild *beasts* at night, indicating
she was getting very little sleep for five months! In the parable of

the man sowing the seed, the fowls of the air attempted to eat the seed before it could be planted in good soil (Matt. 13:4). Christ interpreted the meaning as the birds represented evil spirits that would steal the seed of the Word from a person's heart.

Rizpah refused to allow a single bird to take one piece of her sons' flesh. Birds are also alluded to when Abraham cut covenant with God on an altar where God passed between the pieces. We read, "And when the fowls came down upon the carcasses, Abram drove them away" (Gen. 15:11, KJV). It is unknown why flesh-eating birds are compared to demonic spirits other than demons feed off the flesh (carnal) nature of their victims, and they pick their victims apart, one piece at a time. This is how the adversary sets up his assaults—one at a time, to wear down the one under attack. Someone once said, "I am so beat up emotionally and spiritually that I feel like the vultures are circling." I replied, "That's good!" They looked at me puzzled. I replied, "As long as the vultures are circling you are still alive. I have never seen vultures eat what was living but only what was dead!"

Rizpah remained on the rock for five months or one hundred fifty days. Her unwavering commitment to see her sons' remains cared for was unshakable, as she began her watch in the spring with the barley harvest and stood her ground until the fall months, which is the beginning of the fall rainy season. It was in the time of the rain that David the king heard of her plight and moved on her behalf. Rain is a metaphor for the outpouring of the Holy Spirit (Joel 2:23; Zech. 10:1; Hosea 6:3). It requires the power of the Holy Spirit to break the death spirit and dry spells upon the ones you love. There is no way a person, or a remnant of individuals, can spend day after day in prayer without eventually gaining the attention of the King in heaven, who will move into your situation. Rizpah remained on the rock until the rain came. We need more intercessors to remain on their watches in the mornings and evenings until the atmosphere in their homes and churches change, and the silence is broken by the thundering of God, and the dryness is shattered with the fresh rain of the Holy Spirit.

Those who knew my father, Fred Stone, recall him telling of the great coal field revival, which began when a few older men and women joined together in prayer continually for about six months. A spiritual awakening followed that continued for forty-two months every night, leading to the conversion of hundreds of souls.

Having personally seen tens of thousands come to Christ and nearly ninety thousand baptized in the Holy Spirit, I have discovered the following facts. Most people who came to Christ did so after friends or family members prayed for them consistently. Second, most had a direct encounter with a message or a word from God that convicted them of their sinful lifestyles. And third, they had a face-to-face encounter with the Holy Spirit who directed them to Christ.

Years ago one of our missionaries had been praying for his son to receive Christ. The lad had been into drugs and heavy addictions. The missionary invited his son to join him on a missionary trip to Indonesia, the largest Islamic nation in the world. There is something about seeing the hunger and power of God released upon souls in other nations that often seizes the heart of even the toughest teenager. Upon arriving in the nation, the host minister directed the team to go directly to a poor area and minister to the people, all of whom claimed Islam as their religion. After the missionary spent some time sharing the gospel, the hosts asked his son to pray a prayer for the sick. The young man was hesitant, as he felt unworthy to offer any prayer because his own life fell short of serving Christ. But he began praying, and suddenly a person with a withered hand began screaming as his hand shot out straight!

The visible miracle shook the son to his core, and he fell down repenting and crying out to God. Throughout the entire trip he was seen laying his hands upon people in the streets, hotel lobbies, and anywhere someone wanted prayer! One encounter with the presence of God was all it required to bring a lad to repentance, as it is written, "the goodness of God leads you to repentance" (Rom. 2:4).

CHAPTER 15

BREAKING WITH MOAB TO GET TO BOAZ

THE BIBLE REVEALS AN ENCOURAGING WORD FOR single women, widows, or a woman who has gone through a divorce because of an unfaithful companion. It is the romantic story of Ruth. The narrative of Ruth has all the elements of a giant box-office hit. It contains sudden trouble, tragedy, and death. It has romance, love, and success—a rags-to-riches story. The difference, however, is that it is not fiction, but it is one of the greatest love stories in the Bible. The fields and heritage of Boaz go back to the faith of Rahab and the scarlet thread.

This exciting adventure story will give hope to everyone whose backgrounds challenge their future destinies. It gives hope that no matter what you encounter in life, whether it is famine, death, or lack, God has a progressive plan that moves you from a lack to a lot, from sorrow to success, from fear to faith. God is planning your blessing when you are still walking in the dark of the unknown.

The theme of the Book of Ruth reminds me of the words of Hebrews 10:9, "He takes away the first that He may establish the second." Ruth's first husband died in Moab, but she later found her Boaz. When important things are lost, God can return to you not just what was taken but can also give you better.

When Trouble Strikes

Decisions you make today will affect your life tomorrow. Most choices we make are based on a preconceived idea of an *expected* outcome. We flee conflict and cling to success. To us, it seems impossible that a good God could allow bad things to happen to good people. Jesus noted, however, "Your Father in heaven…sends rain on the just and on the unjust" (Matt. 5:45). The determining factor in surviving the storm is the foundation upon which your faith is built.

Some foundations melt under the pressure of swirling circumstances because the belief system was built on sand, or upon unsustainable and unbiblical expectations. Others can experience the same trouble, stand dripping wet amid deafening thunder and blinding lightning, and still remain firm when the clouds of darkness have lifted, preparing for a new beginning as the day breaks with morning light. The difference is who or what you are trusting and how you react to trouble. The Book of Ruth gives us insight into how people should and should not react when the unexpected happens.

This story begins with two major themes: famine and death. In an effort to flee a terrible famine in Bethlehem, a husband and father named Elimelech packed up his family and migrated to Moab. Living there ten years, he and his two sons, both married to

Moabite women, suddenly died. As if the aching pain of lack was not enough, now the three widows, Naomi, Orpah, and Ruth, were left without men in their lives.

Tragedies such as famine and death move people either closer to God or further from Him. Naomi, for example, was a strong woman who, instead of being humbled, became resentful. Yet the same set of circumstances that brought Ruth into the family would merge into a road of destiny with a royal lineage emerging from her bloodline.

When Naomi and her husband fled with their two sons to escape the famine in Judah, she didn't know that ten years later she would return a broken, depressed, and bitter woman. Who did she feel was responsible for this? Naomi revealed this when she said, "The Almighty has dealt very bitterly with me" (Ruth 1:20). Tragedy had caused her to lose her vision, her purpose, and her concept of God's goodness.

Famine can test your patience in the present, but death can test your truth in God's plan for the future. Too often we blame God for every tragedy that happens, not remembering that death is an enemy of God and came to earth through Adam and Eve's sin. Life, once sweet, can suddenly turn painful. The same sun that melts wax, hardens clay. The victories of today can turn into the sorrows of tomorrow. But if we open our hearts to the story of Ruth, we can understand how God plans His *long-term* purposes, even before the storms of life arrive.

Famines in Strange Places

Throughout the Bible Bethlehem is a special city. Rachel, a matriarch who died in childbirth, was laid to rest on the outskirts of this city after giving birth to Benjamin (Gen. 35:16–20). So from its earliest days this small village has been associated with *death* and *separation*. Yet, the name *Bethlehem* implies blessing. It comes from two Hebrew words, *beyth*, which means, "house," and *lechem*, which means, "bread." Bethlehem was known for its large grain fields, which were divided into sections. Here farmers would harvest barley in the mid to late spring, and wheat in the summer. The grain used to make the bread for the table of showbread in the temple was taken from the fields of Bethlehem. It seems odd that this *house of bread* would experience lack, especially a famine.

Famines are caused by droughts, which in turn are caused by a lack of rain. In a spiritual application spiritual famines are caused by a lack of spiritual rain. When the Holy Spirit is not being poured out in churches, a spiritual famine occurs. There is a famine in the world today—not of bread, but of the Word.

People will eat the strangest things in times of famine. When people get hungry, this causes their flesh to begin to react in strange ways. In some instances mothers were eating their children during a severe famine (2 Kings 6:28–29). Likewise, when a church becomes dry and stagnant without the rain of the Spirit, a famine will ensue, often causing church members to turn on one another. Soon gossip and backbiting become commonplace. In Paul's words, "You bite and devour one another" (Gal. 5:15).

Numbers 11 reveals that the Hebrews grew tired of manna and began to complain. The taste of Egypt was still in their mouths. "Who will give us meat to eat?" they asked (Num. 11:4). To appease the grumblers, God sent quail that accumulated three feet deep in the desert (v. 31)! God allowed them to gorge their flesh by eating flesh. After a period of time judgment fell, and the flesh eaters died in the wilderness (v. 33).

When believers devour one another with cutting words, the entire body of Christ is affected. When people use harsh words to cut and destroy people, the result will be physical sickness. Paul wrote to the Corinthian church and addressed the division and strife among them. Paul revealed:

> For he who eats and drinks in an unworthy manner eats and drinks judgment to himself, not discerning the Lord's body. For this reason many are weak and sick among you, and many sleep.
> —1 CORINTHIANS 11:29–30

During severe droughts and famines, humans have not only devoured other humans, but also things a person would never eat suddenly become appetizing! During a famine in 2 Kings 6:25, people were selling dove's dung and donkey brains in order to survive. Starving people will attempt to survive by eating strange things.

When famine hit Bethlehem, one Jewish family made an unusual move. They crossed the Jordan River into the land of the Moabites. For Elimelech, a Jew, and his family to live in Moab was an unusual occurrence. The Moabites were descendants of an incestuous relationship between Lot and one of his daughters. In fact, the Moabites were placed under a curse by the Law of Moses (Deut. 23:2–4).

So for Elimelech and his family to leave Bethlehem and go to Moab was regression, not progression. But when people are hungry, they will look for bread in unusual places.

When Tragedy Comes in Threes

While in Moab, Naomi's two sons, Mahlon and Chilion, married two Moabite women, Ruth and Orpah. We are uncertain what happened, but both sons died in Moab. Elimelech, Naomi's husband, also passed away. In ancient times there were no government social programs or financial assistance for widows. A woman losing her husband lost more than a companion; she also lost her financial security.

At this point Naomi's future was in jeopardy. Normally when a man passed away, his oldest son would inherit the property and the land. When Naomi's husband died, the inheritance left in Bethlehem was in danger of being claimed by other family members because her sons had also died. Unless something happened, she would lose it all. If she remained in a foreign land, she would have to relinquish all rights to her husband's land.

To have any chance at all of getting her property back, she would have to return to Bethlehem. Even then she would not be able to retain the property for herself. One of her husband's kinsmen would have to step forward and redeem it for her. Naomi was practically destitute.

Staying on the Wrong Side of the River

Some people are said to live *on the wrong side of the tracks*, and Moab was considered to be on the wrong side of the river. Bethlehem was on the west side, and Moab on the east side. The west side was considered blessed, and the east side was under a Mosaic curse. Many people can't see themselves rising above their failures because they have more faith in the *power* of where they came from than faith in the *potential* of where they are going.

Moab was just the wrong place to be from. Even God said so. The Law of Moses said that a Moabite was not to enter the congregation of the Lord up to the tenth generation. The curse had made the Moabites enemies of Israel in the early days.

In order to break the curse, a Moabite had to convert to the God of Abraham, Isaac, and Jacob. This meant they would have to leave their homeland and journey to a place they had never seen. Some were willing to break with everything they had ever known and cross the river of destiny; most, however, continued on in Moab.

When Naomi decided to return to her home, her daughter-in-law, Orpah, chose to remain in Moab. Her choice was a decision to continue in her past. Orpah could sit on the mountainside overlooking Israel in the distance, seeing the hills surrounding Bethlehem, but she never crossed the Jordan. Her life became an existence of memories of death, three funerals, and a mother-in-law and a sister-in-law she would never see again.

Moab is a place of bad experiences and bad memories. In Moab you're always living in the past. The country, Moab, was named after a son of Lot. When Lot fled Sodom with his two daughters, as far as they knew, some scholars think they believed they were the only three left on earth. The daughters, thinking this was the end of humanity in their region, decided to get their father drunk and have sexual relations with him. This, they thought, would ensure that mankind would continue on.

As a result of this scheme, two sons were born. One was named Ben-Ammi, and he was the father of the Ammonites. The other was named Moab (Gen. 19:37–38). As Lot watched Moab grow up, he was constantly tormented by his past. Moab was a living reminder of that terrible night in the cave when, in a drunken stupor, Lot begat a son by his own daughter.

In Moab people are reminded of the one-night stands that birthed the unexpected. Bad things happen in Moab. Three godly men died there. It is a place of sorrow. Linger in Moab, and you are reminded, repeatedly, of past failures, of the affair you had, of the time you turned from God. Thoughts of tragedy and what-ifs haunt you. Moab represents events in your life you'd rather forget.

In Mark 5 the man of Gadara was possessed with two thousand evil spirits. He lived among the tombs; he resided in a graveyard

(v. 3). A graveyard is a place of death. Dotting the landscape of a graveyard are headstones, macabre reminders of a person's past. You see, a graveyard has no future. A cemetery is simply a memorial to a life that used to be. When entering a graveyard, people who are still living spend portions of their time weeping.

Into this kind of environment the devil drove the man of Gadara. He was stranded in the wilderness, living among the ruins of the past. The enemy targets you to stay in Moab. He wants to remind you of your failures. As long as you dwell in the tombs of yesterday, you will not move toward a resurrection of hope in your tomorrows.

Day and night the man in the tombs cried out in torment (v. 5). Do you have restless days and restless nights without relief? Do you cringe in the morning and the evening because your life is at a standstill? Perhaps you can *break chains*, but you cannot get out of the graveyard. You have physical strength, but you are so tormented by the enemy that he paralyzes your spirit.

The tomb is where memories are buried deep in the ground, memories of what could have been if things had turned out differently. Yet what means the most to you is gone from you. Your marriage may be dead, your family may be void of joy, and your job has become a five-day-a-week burden. You are stuck in Moab, living among the tombs!

Moab is a real place. It is where bad things happen to good people. To come into the future blessings of God, you must make a break from Moab. Like the man from Gadara, you must have an encounter with Jesus and come out of the tombs! You must forget those things that are behind and reach forward to those things that are ahead (Phil. 3:13).

No doubt you will encounter obstacles. Moab and Bethlehem are separated by the Jordan River. It must be crossed. It will take faith to leave your past and head toward your future. It will take courage to cross the Jordan River and go into an area of work or ministry you have never known. Friends will tell you to stay where you are, but there comes a time when you must realize God has a divine connection for you in Bethlehem.

Depressed People
Give the Wrong Advice

After all of her troubles in Moab, Naomi finally decided to return home. She would leave her past and go back to Bethlehem (Ruth 1:20–22). Instead of returning home joyously, however, she returned home devastated. Naomi was a strong woman who, instead of being broken, had become bitter.

Naomi's bitterness was obvious in her interaction with those who loved her. It appears that when Naomi began to leave Moab, both Ruth and Orpah decided to leave with her:

> Therefore she went out from the place where she was, and her two daughters-in-law with her; and they went on the way to return to the land of Judah. And Naomi said to her two daughters-in-law, "Go, return each to her mother's house"...And they said to her, "Surely we will return with you to your people."
> —RUTH 1:7–8, 10

Three times Naomi discouraged the girls from going with her to Bethlehem (Ruth 1:8, 11, 13). In fact, the context seems to indicate that she was commanding them not to follow her. She commanded them to go back to Moab and find husbands among their own people. Why did Naomi discourage them? Because she was discouraged! In verses 20 and 21 Naomi revealed her emotional condition:

> But she said to them, "Do not call me Naomi; call me Mara,
> for the Almighty has dealt very bitterly with me. I went out
> full, and the LORD has brought me home again empty."

Naomi was bitter at God for the loss of her husband and two sons. She said, "The hand of the LORD has gone out against me!" (Ruth 1:13). The name *Mara* is a form of the word *marah*. In the wilderness Israel came to the bitter waters of Marah and could not drink until the waters were sweetened. *Strong's Greek and Hebrew Dictionary of the Bible* says the word means "a bitter place in the desert." When Moses threw wood into the bitter water of Marah, the bitterness was made sweet (Exod. 15:22–25). The death of Christ on the cross can take a bitter soul and make it sweet through redemption.

Naomi had been through so much hurt, making her unable to encourage others who were hurting. One who is *whole* needs no physician (Matt. 9:12). It is possible for a healthy person to nurse someone else back to health, but a person who needs a doctor certainly has difficulty healing another. Likewise, a person who is hurting emotionally has bruised faith, limiting his or her ability to minister to others' needs. Bitter people make bitter people more bitter. Angry people make other angry people angrier. Hurting people have difficulty in healing hurting people.

Apparently Naomi had not prayed about God's will for Ruth and Orpah. Chances are she had not consulted the Lord about her own decision. When famine hit Bethlehem, why did her family move to Moab? Did they pray about it? They heard that bread was in Moab, and they reacted to *prevent death*. Yet all three men died in Moab. Now Naomi hears there is bread back home. It seems that the things Naomi heard always moved her. By examining Naomi's reaction to circumstances, we learn two valuable lessons. First, never assume that the obvious thing is the right thing. We should inquire of God's will in every situation. Second, never take advice from a bitter person. He could give you the wrong counsel because his decision making is blurred.

Naomi reasoned, "I cannot have any more sons. If I could, my daughters-in-law would be too old to marry them. Ruth and Orpah need to stay here." Since Ruth and Orpah were familiar and comfortable with Moab's surroundings, Naomi encouraged them to stay put. Naomi wanted to enter Bethlehem alone, depressed, bitter, and defeated in her spirit.

As the story continued to unfold, however, the two young women make two completely different choices. Ruth felt a connection with Naomi. Ruth remembered the joy when Mahlon, Naomi's son, was engaged to her. She recalled Naomi talking about a possible grandson, and describing how the wedding would be a giant celebration.

Ruth knew that Naomi needed inner healing. Ruth knew a little girl with pure faith was locked up inside of this bitter woman who lost her faith. She knew that Naomi longed to have a grandchild bouncing on her knee. Ruth wanted to be a part of Naomi's life. She yearned to see Naomi the way she was before the darts of the triple tragedy of death pierced her soul.

One factor distinguishing Ruth from Orpah was that Orpah was selfish. Perhaps she stayed in Moab, thinking, "If I stay here, I will find the right husband. God can bless me as well in Moab as He can in Bethlehem." Ruth, however, thought of others. She was not headed out of Moab looking for a husband on the other side of the river; she was unwilling to allow her mother-in-law to walk alone. Naomi would become her link to her future.

Ruth saw the situation and sensed something special. She recognized the call to minister to someone. When people receive a *call from God*, most people interpret it as a call for their ministry or a call to use their gift. By contrast, Ruth was called to someone else. It was a burden to move to Bethlehem. It would require her to leave her homeland. She would be separated from childhood friends and loving neighbors. It would mean she would have to walk on strange soil, among strange people with different beliefs and customs. She would live among the Jews, the covenant people of God!

Ruth must have known that Jews were suspicious of strangers. The young Moabite would have to prove herself. Still, she and Naomi had much in common. They were related through marriage. Both had experienced the death of their husbands, and both were leaving the past behind. Orpah, on the other hand, could not make the break.

Daters or Romancers

> Then they lifted up their voices and wept again; and Orpah kissed her mother-in-law, but Ruth clung to her.
>
> —RUTH 1:14

Orpah *kissed* Naomi, but Ruth *clave*. Orpah thought about herself, but Ruth thought about Naomi. Orpah represents the believer whose commitment is not strong enough to break from the past and move into the future. Ruth is the believer whose faith is moving her from the past into the future. Orpah was a woman of *words*, but Ruth a woman of *works*.

On an average Sunday morning there are the *kissers* and the *cleavers*, or the daters and the romancers. Just like a boy dating a girl he is *interested in*, but not in love with, he will show up at his convenience, on his own time and schedule. These Christian daters, if they choose not to sleep in on Sunday, show up just in time and *blow a few kisses* to God with a self-righteous attitude that says, "Lord, aren't You happy that I took time from my busy day to spend one hour with You?" These Sunday-morning-only *saints* are basically interested in enough *fire insurance* to prevent a permanent tour of hell, but they don't have enough faith and love for God to make plans for an eternal destiny in heaven.

Spiritual romancers view their relationship with Christ as exciting, anticipating a week-end in the presence of the Lord. When dating my wife in the early 1980s, I understood the difference between dating and romance. Some men date just to see what they can get out of the other person. Romance requires actions and not mere words. A man of romance will send cards, and not just on special occasions. He will send flowers, speak words of affection, and give undivided attention, holding her hand when walking. A kiss can be an act of the flesh, but romance is a thing of the heart.

When I courted my wife, I wanted to be near her just to hear her speak with her soft, southern, Alabama accent. Looking into her soft, green eyes and holding her hand was, and honestly still is, a thrill. Having her sitting next to me settles my mind and spirit. Before we were married, I often drove ten hours one way just to spend an entire day in the presence of this precious woman. Men who love God will search out a woman like Ruth to become their best friends and companions.

If you are *courting* God for just His blessings, then you are in the *dating* mode. When you are *romancing your lover*, then you can hear an intimate song pouring from your spirit in praise to Him. You will run to your room and open His love letter, the Bible. When you play gospel music, peace will overwhelm your spirit. If He never gave you another blessing, you would love just to feel His presence. Even without earthly blessings, heavenly peace will sustain you.

When Orpah, the dater, kissed her mother-in-law good-bye, she bade farewell to her potential destiny. At the same moment Ruth, the romancer, grabbed Naomi's garment and clung to her side, saying:

> For wherever you go, I will go;
> And wherever you lodge, I will lodge;
> Your people shall be my people,
> And your God, my God.
>
> —RUTH 1:16

What Would You Do to Find God's Will?

How much do you want God's perfect will and direction for your life? Do you desire it enough to spend all night praying? Is it important enough for you to spend several evenings alone in prayer and meditating on God's Word, while others are out having a picnic or sitting in a theater? Do you desire His perfect will to the extent that you would pack up and go where you have never been before?

If necessary would you leave home and the security of those you know to minister to people in a nation to which you have never been? Are you willing to leave your past behind in Moab to journey into the uncharted city of Bethlehem, stepping out on a Word from God as Abraham did—*going but not knowing*? Determination drives you to destiny, which at times means you will stand alone with just you and God.

In my early ministry I spent five years traveling alone to towns I had never been in, staying in homes with families I didn't know. At times I felt I was on an emotional roller coaster because of many disappointing experiences. I remember going to churches to preach revivals, only to discover that the meeting had not even been announced. Posters our office had sent in advance were discarded beneath the pulpit. At times people were uninterested in attending services during the week. I was placed in cold attics and concrete floor basements to stay, and at times had nothing but a bed, table, and a chair in the room. However, my calling was stronger than my discouragement and kept me motivated to fulfill God's will. Knowledge begets confidence, and I knew that I was in God's will.

Discouraged by Family

Have you ever made an exciting announcement that you knew would bring a round of applause from your family, only to watch them act as bored as old paint on a wall. If body language were an actual language, you were just informed to maintain restraint and keep your excitement to yourself. This is how I felt the day I told my father I was called to preach. I had been up most of the night with three other young men praying for revival and experienced a God encounter. I clearly understood the voice of the Holy Spirit saying, "I have called you to preach the gospel." Remember, it is difficult for two people to hear the single voice of God—as Paul heard the voice, and Daniel heard the voice, but those with them had no discernment in seeing and hearing (Dan. 10:7; Acts 9:7). It is difficult to convince a spiritually hearing-impaired believer that God can speak, especially when there is wax built up in the person's inner ear making him dull of hearing.

At times it is difficult for family to believe God has spoken to your spirit, inspired your mind, and revealed His plan when they know better than anyone else your shortcomings, sins, weaknesses, and lack of faith in your past. My earlier days—ages eleven to sixteen—were filled with goofing off, attempting to be a self-made comedian and a practical jokester. If you wanted someone to pull a prank, then pull my string and I would do my thing. I think close friends could not see me serious enough to even put a message together.

My father was the pastor of the church at the time and was a very wise man. Here I was, a kid at age sixteen, and there was Dad, a mature forty-two. His first impression to my announcement was that my four-consecutive-hour prayer meeting had sparked some emotional high that I was caught up in, and I would eventually come down to *reality* and continue my normal schoolboy activities. For once, his discernment failed him on both accounts. I was called, and it wasn't an emotional high; and I never returned to the normal high school kid during my three remaining years of school.

Dad sat in the front pew and watched me preach the first of what would, years later, become tens of thousands of messages. When summer arrived, I invited my granddad to invite me up to his small church in Maryland. This was my first three-day evangelistic crusade with fifteen people, three of whom slept through the entire service. I was rather glad since I stumbled over several biblical words, and those snoring through the message were unaware of my stumbling. Years later Dad expressed his strategy in not being overly supportive to my call to ministry. He knew that many young men had stepped out in zeal, returning home discouraged, hanging up the phone on their alleged call from God. Dad wanted to ensure that my call was not based upon an emotional moment but a true burden for ministry.

My mother always called my dad a pack-rat, as it seemed Dad saved every ministry magazine, filled file cabinets with religious articles, and had compiled a library of hundreds of books. However, his library became my Bible school during my remaining days in high school. After graduating in May, I began traveling to revivals in Mom's borrowed blue Ford, until I made payments on a used green Ford, nicknaming it *The Green Goose*. For some reason it had more speed than the speedometer indicated, as I was pulled over for going too fast seven times in eighteen months and ticketed two times, after reminding the officer I was praying and paying little attention to my speed. Two officers felt I should pray at church, and reminded me by handing me a ticket envelope in which I could send the suggested amount as an *offering* to the courthouse to assist in their *ministry* of protecting the law.

At age sixteen through eighteen I became acquainted with a minister, Emit Hinckley, who was ridiculously talented. He was a master keyboardist, singer, songwriter, an author and ghost writer, publisher, graphic layout specialist, photographer... and did I say a preacher? He rented a building near my house, and I found myself every day just hanging out at the church basement in his print shop, learning how to typeset for a book or magazine, lay it out and print it. I was fascinated with book publishing, and at age eighteen wanted to print my own book. Emit bartered a deal: I would give my drum set to his son, and in return he would print five hundred books for me. My first thirty-two-page booklet, "Precious Promises for Believers," was made available in those early rural revivals for one dollar a copy.

There are three things you should understand about God's will. First, no one can discover or *follow* the will of God like the one who received the revelation of that will. Second, never expect anyone to be as *excited* as you are about what God has planned for you. Third, no one will ever work as hard to *protect* what you personally birth on the same level that you will. When I began sharing with pastors that God had called me to preach, they each had their own perspective of how I should proceed. Because God's process was far different than their expectations, I was labeled a one-year wonder that would soon, like a burning shooting star, be here today and gone tomorrow. I was told, "If you don't follow the system, you will not amount to anything." Moments of discouragement like this are when *the will of God will take you where the words of men will fail you!*

My determination not to become discouraged and drop out of the ministry may be the strength of a scarlet ministry thread that ran through my spiritual DNA. My grandmother's stepfather, R. L. Rexroad, my grandfather, John Bava, and my father, Fred Stone, were all well-established full-gospel ministers. Solomon wrote that a threefold cord is not easily broken (Eccles. 4:12). From the time I was a child, the incorruptible seed of the Word was planted in my mind and spirit, forming a strong cord of faith that was difficult for the adversary to sever.

Often many spiritual battles begin when a child enters the age of accountability, as the people, places, and circumstances around that child begin forming the opinions, values, and paths he or she will choose. However, the positive and negative life incidents can become a part of your personal testimony and serve the kingdom of God.

It was the restlessness of Ruth that motivated her to make a break from the places of familiarity to go to a land of the unknown. Human nature resists change, and the death of a companion initiates the most intense transition a married partner can face. Moab is a comfort zone, while Bethlehem is a challenge for any female Moabite.

When God begins to speak to your spirit and inspire you to new people, a new place, new ministry, or a new relationship, your beginning will be small (Job 8:7) and at times slow, as God never allows more pressure than you can handle. When Ruth joined hands with Naomi, her intent was to assist her brokenhearted mother-in-law in resettling in her hometown after ten years of exile. Without her knowledge, a handsome, wealthy Jewish landowner was preparing for the barley harvest and was in his heart looking for a future wife, but apparently had no interest in the young women in his labor force. *This was because God was saving his heart for a woman he had never met.*

Going but Not Knowing

The unknown is uncomfortable. In my earlier travels my greatest *dread* was to meet people I didn't know, stay in places I had never traveled, and minister in churches where I had never been. It seems God enjoys stretching your faith by surrounding you with the unfamiliar and unknown. When Abraham left his land and relatives, traveling hundreds of miles in caravans, surrounded by towering mountains, he moved forward going and not knowing. God would say, "Stop here," then, "Move on," then, "Camp here," then, "Get up." The trail of Abraham began at the Euphrates River, went down to the river of Egypt, back up to Hebron, Jerusalem, and surrounding areas. The reason for such a widespread journey was not just a place to maintain huge flocks, but everywhere Abraham and his descendants would walk, God promised to give them the land (Deut. 11:24).

If we had total clarity of each detail of our journey, we would be walking by sight and not by faith. After being gone ten years from Bethlehem, things can change. It was a national law in Israel that if a person had lost land through bankruptcy or by poverty, or, in Naomi's case, the death of her husband, that at the end of seven years the land could be redeemed back. But if the redemption did not occur, the property would revert to the closest of kin, who could sell the land or keep it in the family. Thus the intrigue continues.

CHAPTER 16

The BETHLEHEM LOVE TRIANGLE

FRIENDSHIPS IN THE BIBLE WERE FORGED OUT OF COVenants. David and Jonathan, Saul's son, formed a covenant to protect each other. The greatest example of love and friendship among females in the Bible is Naomi and Ruth. When joined with Boaz, we see the Bethlehem love triangle—three individuals connected by covenant. Ruth was guardian of Naomi, and Naomi was the *setup* for Ruth to meet and marry Boaz. Ruth was a Moabite, and by the law should have no favor among the Israelites. However, her narrative demonstrates that God places more value on the deeds and *actions* of a person than on that person's *ancestry*. God's blessings are based upon *love* and not *lineage*.

Once the two widows entered the city gates, old friends began their homecoming welcoming and their questions to get caught up on the ten years Naomi was missing from Bethlehem. I believe she heard such questions as, "Where is your husband?" "What happened to your two sons?" "Who is the girl with you?" "What brought you back to Bethlehem?" If it was today, I can hear some of the more self-righteous saints in the church commenting, "Well, she got out of God's will when she left here, so I am not surprised everything went wrong for her." "It looks like God got her attention by taking what she loved from her." "If she would have stayed here, her husband and kids would still be alive." "She went to Moab, and you know they are cursed, so she placed herself under a spiritual curse." Job found out that even your best friends will always give their opinions as to why bad stuff happens to good people, but good friends are not always right in their perception, for God told Job his friends did not say the right things to him (Job 42:7–10).

One fact is certain: when bad circumstances begin piling up all at once, it can change the tenderness and joy of even the most sensitive and caring person. When Naomi was asked about the past, she told her friends not to call her Naomi (meaning *pleasant*) but to call her *Mara*, which means *bitter* (Ruth 1:20). Notice she *perceived* that it was the Lord who caused her to become bitter. Nowhere in the Scripture does it say the Lord took her husband or that God slew her sons. She assumed the Lord was to blame for her bad circumstances. Job understood that both good and evil happen to all people, and in the early stages of his losses, he said the Lord gave it and took it away (Job 1:21). However, we now know it was a targeted assault from Satan himself (Job 2:1–7). Nothing happens to a believer that surprises God, for the Lord works His plan, turning the bad into good. Bethlehem was the house of bread, a picture of the church. Yet Naomi had lost her identity in the house of bread. She "went out full," but came "home again empty" (Ruth 1:21).

God's house should be a safe house for the wounded. I have known of well-respected Christians in the community who messed up, and their sins became public knowledge, headlining the local papers and the first paragraph of the nightly news. Unless the church members come to their aid and rescue the fallen, it becomes difficult at times for the family members to continue to attend the same church. When they see two people talking, someone peering over the top of his or her glasses, or a group huddled together, the enemy builds the imaginations of these wounded family members to believe that the church members are secretly gossiping about them. To be wounded by the world is expected, but to be wounded within the church is a tragedy.

Let me add an observation here. When the famine struck Bethlehem, *not everyone moved out of the city.* It is apparent that many citizens remained and rode out the season of drought and lack. There is no record that Boaz ever departed from Bethlehem or deserted his family's inheritance, but he stayed until the famine broke. This illustrates two types of reactions when trouble comes: to take *flight* or to stand and *fight.* I once knew a young woman who every time something didn't go her way, or if she had a relationship conflict, her first response was to run away. She was like a rabbit standing still one moment but spooked with every sound the next moment, and jumping from place to place like a frog hopping on hot coals. I told her, "You need to learn endurance through testing and gain patience to stand when the storms are blowing, because once you train your mind to run from trouble, you will be running the rest of your life."

If you have the attitude, "I'm done and getting out," this seed will become an escape mechanism, and when your marriage has disagreements you will make divorce an option, or you will avoid dealing with issues when your kids are in rebellion. You will quit good jobs seeking a pot of gold at the next rainbow, only to be drawn away at the conclusion of life's storms by every new rainbow that's arching over a new location. People never bail out when the surroundings look flawless. Success is a magnet that attracts all types of metal, including odd pieces of scrap metal that need to be melted down and can be reformed into something of value. However, when success turns to struggle, and blessings are on hold, some Bethlehemites sense a *call* to another city, perhaps a trek across the Jordan River to the land of Moab. Naomi left as a mother and returned without sons, left a wife and returned a widow, left with an inheritance of land and returned bankrupt and broken.

Then there was Ruth!

We have no biblical description of her physical appearance, but rabbis assume she would be in her late twenties, perhaps twenty-six to twenty-nine years of age. We can assume that most Moabites had olive-colored skin and dark hair and eyes—as did most of the girls in that region of the world. Once Ruth the Moabite entered the city gates of Bethlehem, she never brought up her past, her departed husband, her lack, or the fact that as a Moabite she was considered a cursed seed in the eyes of Torah-observant Jews. Ruth, at that moment, had no clue that one day her name would be great in Israel and she would be entered into the bloodline of the Messiah. In reality Ruth was the best thing that ever happened to Naomi, and for Boaz, the best thing to ever walk through the city gate!

God's will can only be released when you are in the *right place at the right time* with the *right people*. Years ago one of our youth at our OCI ministry came to me requesting prayer for her sister, a bright young girl who lived in another state and was involved in a same-sex relationship. She had been raised by Christian grandparents, but she had connected with a group whose beliefs were contrary to her upbringing. How do you pray for someone who is enjoying his or her lifestyle with no interest in changing? This is a common dilemma with parents who desire for their children to serve the Lord, but instead they are serving the flesh and feeding off the iniquities of friends. After pondering how to pray, I felt an inspiration.

I said, "The only way such a relationship can be broken is if we pray that the Lord permits confusion to come and break the emotional ties." We began to ask God to break the emotional and physical ties between these two women and allow there to be confusion and strife within their relationship. This seems an odd way to pray, but within a few weeks the two were arguing and almost violently disagreeing. It took eighteen months of praying and believing God, but the young woman broke off the relationship, moved, and is now serving God. Many times when two people break an emotional tie with sexual activity and strong feelings, the adversary will work against their minds and tell them to take their own lives now that it's all over and there is no one left to love them. This is the enemy attempting to keep you in Moab—the place of death and negative memories.

Never pray for God's will to be done, then become angry when something didn't go your way. If your way is the wrong way then God is going to open up another way. He will not perform an autopsy on your opinion concerning His decision before He acts. The person or people entering your life today may be exiting your life in twelve months. That attraction can become a distraction, and it requires action to dislodge people who are blocking your forward movement from one location to the next.

Moab is a land of mountains, and Bethlehem was surrounded by mountains, but not all mountains are the same. It's what lies in the *valley* between the mountains that matters. In the case of Ruth and Naomi, in the valley was the huge grain field owned by Boaz. Naomi changed mountains and found her healing, and Ruth found her destiny in a fertile valley between the Judean hills—the fields of Boaz.

The Progression of the Blessing

When God is preparing to bless you, He will always send a person into your life. Naomi's connection was Ruth, and Ruth's connection would be Boaz—a triangle of three who would be bonded by love. Ruth 4:21 indicates that the father of Boaz was Salmon, who was married to Rahab. The miracle of the scarlet thread that spared her entire family was continuing the covenant blessing into the life of her son. Timing is a key to divine direction. In the case of Ruth and Naomi, it was the season of the barley harvest (Ruth 1:22), which begins at the time of Passover when a firstfruit of barley is marked and cut. Boaz was a near relative to Naomi's dead husband:

> There was a relative of Naomi's husband, a man of great wealth, of the family of Elimelech. His name was Boaz.
>
> —RUTH 2:1

Naomi had never told Ruth about Boaz, as originally she instructed Ruth to remain in Moab and never said, "Come with me; I have a rich friend you need to meet." Ruth's motives for joining with her mother-in-law were pure and sincere—to convert to her God and to care for her. There are times some individuals set out to connect with someone hoping for blessing by association, or to build their own reputations by connecting to someone who has one. True servants avoid the publicity and prefer their rewards to be given for their private work and not for public accolades.

As a single teenage traveling minister, it didn't take long to get lunch or early dinner invitations from some very spiritual mothers or grandmothers who just happened to be praying for a daughter or granddaughter to find a young husband—especially a *young preacher*. When I met my future wife, Pam, a single teenager from Alabama, one characteristic that impressed me was her pure motives. She really had no visions or dreams of marrying any young preacher or being a minister's wife. In fact, she told me for years that she didn't feel like she had the formal training to be a minister's wife. In the four-week revival where we met, I can still recall about three young girls who felt they could be in line as a candidate for a minister's wife. It was not because I was some handsome Italian stallion. Quite the contrary, I was a skinny, pale-skinned, black bushy-haired Virginia boy. However, the preaching and anointing were appealing to some.

In those days yearly camp meeting was a time and place for young people to meet. Sometimes young girls competed with one another to see who could go out with one of the many young ministers who were state evangelists at the time. This was disturbing because some of the girls were only interested in being able to say, "I went out with so and so," and were not interested in the minister as a person.

Like Ruth, my Pam had different, purer motives. When I told her I loved her, she shared it with only her two sisters and the lady she and her sisters were living with. People in her church had to question her about how I was doing and how I felt about her. She was very private and personal about our conversations and our relationship. Like Mary, Pam hid her feelings and dreams in her heart. She was not looking for a preacher, but she got one. One reason I was so attracted to her was because she was not chasing every young man who crossed her path. She had no desire to become a preacher's wife. She had no selfish motive about our relationship. She was in love with Perry Stone, the man, not just Perry Stone, the preacher.

To this day she continues to minister behind the scenes with her gentle spirit. She homeschools, takes care of our personal finances and bills, works at the VOE and OCI ministry offices, cooks for the conferences, just to name a few of the things she does. Some women and men are like an ever-running faucet of water—they talk endlessly about everything, never keeping a confidence. They feed their egos by wanting others to know how much they know. With women, the Bible calls them "silly women" who run from house to house telling everything they know about everybody they know (2 Tim. 3:6, KJV). That is not what God needs or what a man desires in a woman.

God wants women who, like Ruth, have a gentle and quiet spirit, one in whom a person can confide (1 Pet. 3:4). Personal information can be power in the wrong hands. People will never trust a gossip with private information; they will trust only women like Ruth who are peaceable, gentle, and do their jobs without complaining.

Boaz was a special man who needed a special woman. Boaz was a strong leader. He did not need a strong female personality beside him to compete with. Boaz knew what he was doing. He needed a woman like Ruth, who was willing to work alongside him as he pursued the will of God for himself and his family.

At age eighteen I was in full-time evangelism. Pastors informed me I needed a piano-playing singer to accompany me as a wife. It took me three years to realize I didn't need a wife who was talented in a church service; I needed a wife who could take care of me. I needed a comforting voice when the message I preached didn't go well, when the crowds were down and the altars were empty, when the offerings wouldn't pay the bills, and the journey back home was long and difficult; a song and a piano wouldn't suffice. I realized I needed a wife who would hold my hand, snuggle next to me, and say, "Hey, babe (Pam's favorite saying to me), I'm with you, and I know God is going to take care of us."

I needed an encourager. Ruth's very presence made Naomi feel better. Ruth would not hurry, but she had the patience to wait for God's will. The Bible reveals that Ruth knew how to respect and respond to a man. I concluded that this was also what I needed in a wife.

The Threefold Progressive Blessing

Naomi returned to her city in the time of the barley harvest (Ruth 1:22). She was in the right place at the right time. Bethlehem, the house of bread, was known for its fields of barley and wheat. The seven feasts of Israel revolve around the times of harvesting. The Feast of Passover falls during the barley harvest, while the Feast of Pentecost falls during the wheat harvest. If you're looking for bread, go to where grain is being harvested!

There in Bethlehem Ruth discovered a progression in the blessing of God. Searching the Scriptures, it is clear that God's favor comes to those who are obedient in little things (Matt. 25:21–23). Once we learn to walk through the small doors, God will open up larger ones for us.

The movement and progression of our blessings are dependent on our last act of obedience. God only releases the next blessing when we follow through with the last instruction.

Though she was from Moab, Ruth understood the principles of God. She knew that in order to obtain success, you must have two elements working on your behalf. Ruth asked for *grace* (Ruth 2:2, KJV) and for *favor* (v. 13). Favor opens the door, but grace keeps the door open! Ruth submitted to Naomi's advice and was willing to serve without recognition.

One of the lesser taught principles discovered in Ruth's narrative is the New Testament principle Christ taught of the thirtyfold, sixtyfold, and hundredfold blessing (Mark 4:3–8). Having stood in Galilee where this message was preached, I can visualize the effect it had on the people there. In this open-air setting Christ spoke about a man planting seed. Today there is a large farm at the base of the hill where Jesus preached, and wheat is grown there.

Jesus spoke of seeds falling on the stones. In this section of Galilee there are countless black basalt stones covering the ground that must be removed before farmers plant any fields, or else the seed will never take root and will dry and die on the rock's surface.

In the parable birds swoop down and eat the small seeds before they can take root. I have personally observed a farmer in Galilee plow a field and begin planting seed in the field. Hovering above him were numerous birds that would actually land in the fresh soil, looking perhaps for worms or possible seeds. Birds must be swooshed away to prevent them from controlling the field.

In the parable the heat of the sun can beat down on the seed, and if the seed is not covered with soil, or if rain ceases to moisten the ground, drought can produce dry seasons, and dry seasons can bring crop failure.

As Jesus preached the parable of the sower, He painted a beautiful illustration for His listeners. Everything He spoke about could be seen before the eyes of the people. Jesus then revealed that if the seed of the Word took root, it would always produce. In fact, it would produce "some thirtyfold, some sixty, and some a hundred" (Mark 4:8).

The level of blessing is not measured solely by the amount of seed planted, but it is also determined by the condition of the soil or the heart of the person receiving the Word. The story of Ruth reveals the threefold level of increase upon those who are willing to hear, plant, and obey the Word of God.

The Principle of Increase

> For the earth yields crops by itself: first the blade, then the
> head, after that the full grain in the head. But when the
> grain ripens, immediately he puts in the sickle, because the
> harvest has come.
> —Mark 4:28–29

This scripture reveals the principle of the increase of thirty, sixty,
and hundredfold increase. Notice the threefold process of a single
seed placed in the soil:

- First comes the *blade*

- Then the head or the *ear* and stalk

- Followed by the *full grain*, the corn or mature grain

The blade represents the first level, the thirtyfold level; the stalk
represents the sixtyfold level; and the mature fruit represents the
complete hundredfold level. Once the seed reaches maturity and
becomes a ripe ear, then it can be picked from the stalk and eaten,
or the seeds on the ear can be used and planted for a future harvest.
One ear of corn can produce dozens of plants, which can, in turn,
produce hundreds of ears.

People can *eat* their seed or *replenish* it by planting from the
previous harvest for a future harvest. People who are not givers will
always eat their seed. They live for the now and not for tomorrow.
Since the story of Ruth shows the miracle of increase, the three
stages of growing can be observed in Ruth's life. Applying this pattern to Ruth, we see her beginning in the *corner* of the field as the
blade. Her *handfuls of purpose* are the *stalk*. But when Boaz *laid it
on her* she received an overflow, far above what she had anticipated
(Ruth 3:15).

Moving From the Seed to the Mature Fruit

I believe each year that passes you should always be increasing in some area of your job, church, family, and spiritual growth. I am familiar with a major denomination that over the years has shut down all their Christian bookstores, their major printing presses that were once used for songbooks and other gospel literature, and has cut back the budgets for youth and missions. This is very sad, as the world is in the greatest season of soul harvest among the nations, and we need to advance the kingdom in preaching, teaching, and the printed word.

For the individual, instead of waiting for some type of dream door to open that will thrust you into a Cinderella-type destiny, you should step into any and every opportunity available to minister to whomever you can. Since age eighteen I have conversed with hundreds of young people who felt a *call* into the ministry. I have shared my personal testimony with them and encouraged them to pursue the inner desire they felt.

Sometimes I would return to the church years later to find that they were still waiting for the Lord to *open the door*. When reminding them that the local jail, nursing home, or their own church's bus ministry provides an opportunity for them to minister, some would reply, "That's not my call. I am called to preach behind a pulpit."

I eventually realized they were not actually called to preach. They were fired up with zeal to do something for God, but in their minds they have limited their *calling* to a pulpit. Preaching behind the pulpit is the most common type of ministry. However, Jesus said to "go into all the world and preach the gospel" (Mark 16:15). Almost 90 percent of all preachers worldwide live in America. Why don't some of those who want to preach go out where the harvest is? The will of God is not fulfilled by dreaming but by doing.

In the late 1980s I conducted a yearly revival at the Upper Room Church in Orange County, California. There I met a young man named Jonathan Augustine. Jonathan attended the revival every night faithfully. In the course of the meeting I discovered that every weekend he would head out to a large youth hangout and preach on the street to the young people. Often he was mocked, laughed at, and criticized, but he would not hold back because the Word of God burned in him like a fire.

I told his pastor, the Reverend Floyd Lawhon, that God was going to use this young man because he was faithful in the little things. At the revival during a special service, the bishop of a large denomination in Bulgaria spoke at the church before I ministered. He invited anyone who felt a burden to come to Bulgaria and minister.

Jonathan felt the burden and the urge to travel to Bulgaria. He packed up and set off for Bulgaria, and he ended up staying for several months. Miraculously the Lord began to give him the ability to speak the Bulgarian language. He eventually took a small church and built it up to about five hundred people. He returned to America to further his education, and he eventually met a lovely Bulgarian girl. They were married, and today they have a handsome son. He and his wife are now overseeing a Bible school where he serves as a regional overseer in a section of Europe, and they are making a powerful impact on lives in Eastern Europe! What Jonathan has accomplished began with a small dream seed—planted in fertile soil. As he obeyed the Lord, that single seed began to sprout, until now a great harvest has been realized. The dream represents a thirtyfold level, the sprouting was sixtyfold, and the harvest is one hundredfold.

In your own field of labor, the roots of inner conflicts, such as bitterness and unforgiveness, must be uprooted out of your spirit. The large stones that are stumbling blocks must be plucked out of your field, ensuring the seed will take root without hindrances. The seed-choking junk in the soil of your heart today will become the hindrance of your life tomorrow.

The Law of Gleaning

There are circumstances in life we cannot control. We have no field of labor to call our own, no seeds to plant, and no harvest to reap. We lean upon the faith and compassion of others undergirding us, carrying us through difficult times. This was Ruth's situation. However, God in His wisdom established a law in the Torah to assist those in dire circumstances—the Law of Gleaning.

This law was applied especially to the barley, wheat, and grape harvests. When a farmer harvested his field, the four corners were untouched so that the poor, the widows, and the strangers could "glean" in the field (Lev. 19:9–10). As a poor stranger Ruth went out in accordance with the law and custom to glean in the fields of Boaz. Notice the divine setup in the location of her gleaning.

> Then she left, and went and gleaned in the field after the reapers. And she happened to come to the part of the field belonging to Boaz, who was of the family of Elimelech.
>
> —RUTH 2:3

Ruth was a stranger from Moab, and during her first days in Bethlehem she was permitted to glean the corners of the barley fields. Ruth was so focused that she didn't have the time for additional social activity. Normally at the conclusion of the day the male reapers and the young ladies would gather for fellowship. It was at one of these moments that Boaz spoke to Ruth:

Let your eyes be on the field which they reap, and go after them. Have I not commanded the young men not to touch you? And when you are thirsty, go to the vessels and drink from what the young men have drawn.

—Ruth 2:9

It appears that two characteristics captured the attention of Boaz: Ruth's work ethic (her focus on her assignment) and her beauty. Ruth was unmarried, and Boaz ensured that no other man would approach her about forming a relationship with her. She gleaned from morning to evening (v. 7), which by Jewish reckoning would be about twelve hours (sunrise to sunset). When she was given a break, she spent a "little" time in the house (v. 7). It may be easy to find a physically attractive woman, but can a godly Boaz find a woman sharing in common interest, an untiring laborer in the harvest field?

I accepted my God-ordained life assignment to minister at age sixteen. From that moment my interests changed as I became disconnected with all public school activities. I had little or no normal social life, remaining in an office or my bedroom, studying for hours without a break. At the time I was not evangelizing, traveling, or preaching. However, during this time, I was learning, like David, to defeat bears and lions in personal, private battles.

It would be some time before there was a Goliath to slay that would launch my ministry into the public eye. (See 1 Samuel 17.) Yet Christ knew my sincerity, determination, and desire to reach out, preach, and see lives changed. I was so focused on the harvest fields where I ministered, and I didn't want to be distracted from my mission. Those years of almost complete isolation have ceased. I now have a beautiful wife, a son and daughter. God has blessed this ministry to reach millions of people around the world. Early focus, spending years alone with God each day, was the seed that grew into a seven-point outreach ministry that reaches two hundred forty-nine nations.

You cannot move toward a *dream* without *steam*—energy from hard work, and unction from the Spirit. Once the dream begins coming to pass, it requires the right *team*. Pastors of great churches have told me for many years that their greatest challenge is to employ individuals who can see the same dream and work with the same intensity that they see and work with. Some workers work on the thirty-, sixty-, and hundredfold work levels. From some you get 30 percent work during the day as they float from place to place, waste time in worthless conversations, take as much time as they want for lunch, and always need to be followed up with as they never follow instructions. The only fruit they bear is the kind they bring to work to eat for lunch. These are the ones whose favorite statement is, "That's not my job." The 60 percenters are good from morning to sometime past lunchtime. Their motivation begins wavering about one in the afternoon, and their best work occurs about five hours out of eight. These are usually good people, but they want out the moment the clock strikes five. The hundredfold are not just on time to work, they also work nonstop and do their assignments, and they look for any other work needed for the day. They are loyal to God, to the minister and the ministry, and to the pastor and the church. In my ministry I have a few individuals whom others have attempted to hire, even offering them more income. They have turned it down and said, "We are called to Perry's ministry, and we are doing the will of God and will stay where we have been planted."

Some employees think they are just biding time until something better comes. However, if you are not working hard in your little corner, you won't work hard in the bigger field. Your work ethic is built on little doors and not big opportunities. Jesus taught,

"And if you have not been faithful in what is another man's, who will give you what is your own?" (Luke 16:12). If you are faithful in the little things, God will make you a ruler over many (Matt. 25:23). If you can't manage one McDonalds, don't expect to have a chain of five that you own in the future. If you can't keep up with the money at a convenience store cash register, don't expect to handle tens of thousands of dollars each week. Businessmen, such as Boaz, are always looking for workers who will *work*. Ruth was a dedicated worker. Remember, except for the grain she collected, she was receiving no compensation for her work! In fact, the portion of grain she collected was taken home to Naomi. She was working in the fields to provide for the need of one who was unable to work—Naomi.

When will we learn that God rewards those who work faithfully and with pure motives (Heb. 11:5)? A recent survey reported that only 19 percent of the working people in America are completely happy in their field of labor.[1] It doesn't take a genius to figure out that 81 percent must be working out of necessity, getting a paycheck to pay bills and provide for the family. This unhappiness with work brings up the question, "Is there not a better way to make a living?"

If we follow the leading of God's Spirit, we could all be laboring in a field that is challenging but fulfilling. Some may be in the right place and just don't realize it, due to a lack of success or results. Just as with your spiritual walk, succeeding in your dreams and visions requires steadfastness and determination. It is impossible to continually plant seeds without eventually getting a harvest. I once said to a person we were hiring in our office, "I compensate people according to the problems they solve, and not the problems they create." If you desire to move up in your job and operate in increase, then let your supervisor see that you have a desire to help the company *increase*. A true servant always considers others before considering themselves.

When You Get Out of Your Corner

Some people have a spirit that says, "I have my own plans and agendas. I have my own ministry." It's me, me, me! Their self-centered lifestyles soon become evident as they begin to pull away from their God-appointed job or ministry in order to pursue their own self-appointed activities.

In contrast some labor faithfully in their appointed duties. Perhaps you are one of these. Most of the time it seems your labor goes unnoticed and your efforts unrewarded. Your level of blessing may be at thirtyfold. You may be in an isolated corner of the harvest field where it seems no one is paying attention. Yet you are working and striving because you are dedicated to your post. You are more concerned with the right actions than others' attention.

At times you are ministering to a Naomi, someone hurting who needs you near them. Your vision and future are inconsequential; your heart is connected with changing the heart of another. Boaz (a type of Jesus) set you into a place of the thirtyfold level. He observes you in the corner at the same time, protecting you from the wrong men and women. He is providing for you because you are in *His* field!

The thirtyfold level is the gleaning level. Keep the faith, for you will not always be in the corner alone, working for someone else. God will mark you for increase. When Boaz began to recognize Ruth's presence, she asked a question.

> Why have I found favor in your eyes, that you should take notice of me, since I am a foreigner?
> —RUTH 2:10

Boaz's answer reveals how the Lord looks on those who minister to others in need. Ruth had three marks against her. She was a *woman*, she was a *Moabite*, and she was a *widow*. She lost her financial security when she lost her husband, she lost her identity when she left Moab, and being a woman made her vulnerable. Most women in her situation would be out searching for a husband who could bring security and meet her needs. Not Ruth! She was different, and that was the very reason Boaz took notice of her.

> And Boaz answered and said to her, "It has been fully reported to me, all that you have done for your mother-in-law since the death of your husband, and how you have left your father and your mother and the land of your birth, and have come to a people whom you did not know before."
>
> —RUTH 2:11

Ruth had no ulterior motive to work at the level she did except to be an encouragement to her mother-in-law. The entire time she was secretly being watched and admired by a single rich man. In the Book of Esther, Esther's beauty is admired, but with Ruth, Boaz admired her concern for another after leaving her mom, dad, and the land of her birth. Boaz spoke a prophetic blessing over Ruth:

> The LORD repay your work, and a full reward be given you by the LORD God of Israel, under whose wings you have come for refuge.
>
> —RUTH 2:12

Notice the phrase "full reward." In the New Testament the phrase "full reward" would be classified as "a great recompense."

> Cast not away therefore your confidence, which hath great recompense of reward.
>
> —HEBREWS 10:35, KJV

The Greek word *recompense* is *misthapodosia*; a word used for a reimbursement. As an example, if you were on a business trip and paid out of pocket for your lodging, food, and gas, you could turn in the receipts and receive a reimbursement from your company. Boaz knew God was the paymaster and would repay Ruth for her labor, just as God will reward those who diligently seek Him (Heb. 11:6).

Favor Moves You Forward

Ruth then said to Boaz, "Let me find favor in your sight" (Ruth 2:13). Favor is special recognition that moves you toward good things. In response Boaz invited Ruth into the workers' house where she sat at the table with all the reapers and ate the food prepared from Boaz's table. The Bible says, "She ate and was satisfied" (v. 14). By gleaning in the corner of the field alone, she was experiencing a thirtyfold level of blessing. This is the level of just enough. Living at thirtyfold is just enough to meet basic needs, just enough to get through, and just enough for your daily bread. Most believers live at this level. Once the monthly bills are paid, there is nothing left over to bless others or even to invest in for the future.

Ruth was a servant working in the corner of the harvest field, but she had the attention of Boaz. She gleaned just enough to meet her need, but God had something more for her. Boaz was ready to give her a promotion.

Be encouraged to know that someone near you has the ability to give you a promotion. Take strength in the fact that there is someone who will move you from the level where you are to a level of increase. Everyone starts in a gleaning corner, but with Boaz on your side, you are going to come out of the corner to a sixtyfold and go into a higher level of blessing.

Moving to a Sixtyfold Level

The next day Ruth arose to perform her daily routine. On this day, however, a special, unexpected blessing awaited her.

> And when she rose up to glean, Boaz commanded his young men, saying, "Let her glean even among the sheaves, and do not reproach her. Also let grain from the bundles fall purposely for her; leave it that she may glean, and do not rebuke her."
>
> —RUTH 2:15–16

Boaz was breaking tradition. Strangers were allowed to glean only in a small corner after the main harvest was completed. Every stranger and widow in Bethlehem was permitted by the Law of Moses to glean a corner. But Boaz got Ruth *out of the corner*, and Boaz instructed, "Do not reproach her…do not rebuke her."

Had the reapers seen Ruth among the sheaves, they would have said, "What are you doing here? This is off limits to you, a stranger and a Moabite." They would have reminded her that her past and her birth place hindered her progress. But Boaz instructed the men to leave her alone. Don't rebuke her, he said, don't bring up the fact she is a stranger among us; make her comfortable. Let *"handfuls of purpose"* fall where she is gleaning (v. 16, KJV)!

Satan is the accuser of the brethren (Rev. 12:10). When he reminds us of our past, it hinders our progress into the future. Often condemning feelings of guilt cloud our vision. People say, "If I had only done this," or "If I hadn't done that." But God is in the *now*! Hebrews 11:1 says: *"Now* faith is…." (emphasis added). Satan cannot determine your future, so he tries to make you a prisoner of your past. When we live in the graveyard of the past, Satan torments us!

Boaz wanted to be sure Ruth's *past* was not an issue as she moved forward into the blessings prepared for her! He had marked the very spot where she had labored. When she was looking away, reapers would throw sheaves of grain on the ground near her feet—a sign of favor. The boss was recognizing her hard work and the commitment she had made. She didn't ask, and she didn't have to work harder, yet she received a recompense for her efforts.

Blessed on Purpose

Boaz was blessing her on purpose! He was telling her, "You are a special person, and I want to show you my appreciation for your spirit and your attitude."

I direct a major ministry. We have full-time workers who assist us in ministry. Some work in meeting planning, some in television video outreach, others answer mail, lay out the magazine, take phone orders, or assist in the prayer ministry, singing, and so forth. For the past thirty-six years we have had numerous people connected to our ministry, both in the office and on the road. There are some who are gone at five and head home, and others who will also clock out but go above and beyond their call of duty. When I see workers staying after normal business hours without being asked, searching to find something they can do, both Pam and I have a desire to bless them beyond what the ministry is doing.

After thirty-six years of full-time ministry Pam and I have observed two types of people: those who come to be a blessing, and those who want a blessing. Some attach themselves to the work for what the ministry can do for them, as others seek what they can do for the ministry. Local churches and ministries need workers who will carry the weight of the ministry. Pastors do not need an associate pastor on staff or members who use the local church as a stepping-stone to later split the congregations and birth their own church three miles down the road out of a rebellion. Pastors need men and women who say, "I am with you, and I am connected to the vision of the house and the ministry; we are a team." As a team you stand together in battles and rejoice together in victories. When a pastor unites a team with this attitude, he would keep them in the game.

Evangelistic ministries need people who are called to that ministry. Those organizations need people who will say, "If I never preach at your camp meeting, I am called. If I never sing before thousands, I am called. If you never brag on my ability, I am with you all the way!"

Ruth was called, and she was chosen. She was a woman of destiny, and she wasn't lazy. God doesn't choose lazy people to minister. He never invites a couch potato into the harvest field. Moses was a shepherd of forty years, and David was busy protecting sheep before he went to battle with Goliath. Levi left his busy tax collector's booth, while Peter was a fisherman who spent entire nights on the sea. God not only recognized the gifting in each person, but He also recognized their bold character and willingness to work.

All who have a worldwide ministry are almost obsessed with their desire to reach the lost. Paul talked about being addicted to the gospel (1 Cor. 16:15). God calls men who will *work* to catch fish and harvest the souls. Jesus may be asking, "Why have you been standing here idle all day?" (Matt. 20:6). Younger ministers visit our ministry headquarters, touring three large buildings, a ranch, and a prayer barn and are at times enamored with the facilities. What they can't see is the prayer, fasting, study time, and nonstop ministry that birthed, grew, and sustained the entire ministry. It is impossible for them to transport back into the past to the bedroom in my father's old house where it all started thirty-six years ago. Each new level requires following a new vision, engaging in new battles, and experiencing new things.

Ruth went into the field every day. As the midday sun beamed rays of unbearable heat on her face, she labored. It was Boaz who invited her into the house for rest. She didn't ask for anything, she just did her job. She arose early and stayed out until the sunset. Boaz, and God, recognized her hard work.

Men of vision promote those of like vision. Boaz's life centered around his vision of a yearly barley harvest. His annual income was wrapped up in baskets of grain collected from the fields. To touch the heart of Boaz, you had to show him how faithful you were in the field! The Lord is looking for people who will love souls and minister to the poor. The Bible says whoever ministers to the poor "lends to the LORD" (Prov. 19:17). The Lord will reward those who seek the harvest first!

> Seek first the kingdom of God and His righteousness, and all these things shall be added to you.
> —MATTHEW 6:33

Ruth moved to the next level of increase. It was the sixtyfold level, between thirtyfold and one hundredfold. It is better than thirty, but not quite as good as one hundredfold. It is *increase*, nonetheless. Tangible blessings were beginning to flow. She was working at the same pace, yet she was receiving additional handfuls on purpose.

Scripture says she gleaned an "ephah of barley" (Ruth 2:17). An *ephah* was approximately five gallons, much more than she had before. When she went into the city to show Naomi, the Bible says, "So she brought out and gave to her what she had kept back after she had been satisfied" (v. 18). Prior to this, she had just enough, but now she had *enough and then some*! As my friend Jentezen Franklin has said, "God is all sufficient. He is *El Shaddai* and not *El Cheapo*."

The Will of God—Increase

The Lord is a God of increase. Before attacking Job, Satan recognized the blessings of the Lord on everything Job touched. Satan said, "His possessions have increased in the land" (Job 1:10). The enemy recognizes progress and increase. The devil knows that your increase means you will have a realm of influence. Your influence can affect the decisions of others.

People listen to those who have influence. Successful people listen to those with a testimony of *how* success came to them. They know that results come only through tests and trials! The biblical principle is that great testing comes before great blessing.

- Moses dwelt in a wilderness watching sheep forty years before pastoring Israel.

- David encountered Ziklag, where he and six hundred men lost everything, before he took the throne.

- Ruth lost her husband before she met Boaz.

But God is a God of increase! He will never leave you with less. It may seem that you are on a decline and that you have less than ever before. But can you be determined like Ruth? Can you work alone in the gleaning corner? Can you minister to another's needs and ignore your own? Can you enjoy isolation from friends and family, knowing that God will eventually increase you?

Many scriptures speak about increase. (See Psalm 115:14; Proverbs 13:11; 1 Corinthians 3:6; 1 Thessalonians 3:12.) The widow in 2 Kings 4 was about to lose her home and two sons to her creditors. But a prophet of God had a plan, and God had the provision. A supernatural oil supply broke forth in her home. She was able to sell the oil to pay her bills. That is *enough*! But then she was told to "live on the rest" (v. 7). That is increase!

The sixtyfold level is the ability to meet your needs and have something left over! God has promised to supply our need, but don't be satisfied with merely having your needs met. Get excited about the possibility of having enough and then some!

Moving to the Highest Level of Blessing

The highest level of blessing is the hundredfold level. This represents the level of total provision, as well as the level where you become a blessing to others. It is the realm of increase to where your "cup runs over" (Ps. 23:5). It is where you are blessed in order to be a blessing.

When Boaz is with you, you will eventually move to the highest level of increase, the hundredfold level! When Ruth showed Naomi how she was blessed, Naomi asked who was helping her and bringing about this increase. Ruth informed Naomi that her benefactor was Boaz. Naomi was thrilled because Boaz was her near kinsman—a relative of Naomi's deceased husband.

It was a divine setup. It was a prearranged God moment. Ruth was unaware of God's purpose for her. She did not move to Bethlehem with a preconceived idea, saying, "I can get a rich Jew to marry me and provide for me." In fact, most Jews of that day would never have considered marrying a foreign woman. It would have been a disgrace for them to marry outside their own race.

God's law was so strict that even the high priest was not permitted to marry a Jewish woman who had divorced or who was widowed unless her previous husband had been a priest. Ruth must have known the odds were against her, but God had a plan. Ruth was willing to believe in the God of Naomi, and God was willing to use this woman because she acted in faith.

Though your beginning was small,
Yet your latter end would increase abundantly.

—Job 8:7

When God blesses you, He has your future in mind. We live a day at a time, but God is visionary. We pray, "Give us our daily bread," and cannot peer into the future to determine where we are going. But God's blessings are for our future. He who is "declaring the end from the beginning, and from ancient times things that are not yet done" has already seen the future (Isa. 46:10).

A Spark of the New Hope

When Naomi heard that Boaz had noticed Ruth, a new hope sprang forth in her heart. When Naomi's husband died, she lost the family property in Bethlehem. The land remained in the name of the husband and was passed on as an inheritance to the oldest son. Because of her sons' deaths, however, there was no one to claim the inheritance. God had established a law of redemption. If a woman lost her husband and had no children, she was to marry a brother of the deceased so she could have sons to carry on her husband's name. If there was no brother to marry, she could redeem her property back through the process of the kinsman-redeemer. A kinsman-redeemer was a next of kin who could, through a legal rite at the gate of the city, redeem the lost inheritance back to its original owner. In this case the original owner was Naomi. Boaz was the kinsman-redeemer. As Ruth continued to labor in the field, God's perfect plan began to come into focus.

[Boaz] also said to me, "You shall stay close by my young men until they have finished all my harvest."

—Ruth 2:21

233

Don't leave your divine appointment too early. When you are talented and dedicated to God, you will gain the attention of people in other fields. From other churches you will hear, "We need you here." They will try to impart their vision into you and say, "You can be more effective with us. We are a larger ministry and a larger church. Think of the results you can have in our field!" You must stay in the area God has placed you until the end of the mission. An early departure may result in an aborted destiny. Naomi encouraged Ruth, "It is good, my daughter, that you go out with his young women, and that people do not meet you in any other field" (v. 22).

All fields are not the same. All churches are not the same. All ministries are not the same. Ruth could have jumped from field to field, but she remained true to one person, Boaz. People often move prematurely. I tell pastors, "Never leave your church when you are discouraged; leave when everything is great." Men leave thinking the grass is greener on the other side only to discover that sheep leave manure in every field!

People get frustrated and disgusted and begin to retaliate against those they are close to and say, "I'll show them; I'll change churches. I'll show them; I'll go somewhere else." They leave before the appointed time and wind up miserable, missing the many blessings God had reserved for them.

Years ago my father pastored a wonderful church in Virginia. Two members gave him problems, but the rest of the congregation were jewels. Dad allowed those two men to discourage him until he reached the point of deciding to move. He ended up going to five different churches over a period of about twelve years. These were good churches and good people, but he was never again fulfilled in pastoring.

He often said, "I should have waited on the Lord. I should not have been so hasty." Never make a decision to change the fields of labor just because another offer seems better, or because you are tired of where you are. Your blessing can only continue when you are where the Holy Spirit wants you.

Following Right Instructions

Ruth received instructions well. She knew how to listen to those who had experience in their realms of expertise. She continued to work in the fields of Boaz.

> So she stayed close by the young woman of Boaz, to glean until the end of barley harvest and wheat harvest; and she dwelt with her mother-in-law.
>
> —Ruth 2:23

Don't jump from assignment to assignment. Don't go from church to church, attempting to find the perfect pastor. Don't run from ministry to ministry, looking for your blessing. Where has God planted you? Where does the anointing flow the best? More money or a better position is not always God's will. It is imperative to be in the right place at the right time! Seeing the potential for increase, Ruth refused to move to another field where she would have had to return to gleaning in a corner. In Boaz's field she was seeing progression and favor from the head man. She was moving toward her destiny and must have sensed that something good was in the works.

Still, she knew it would require time. She knew she had to wait in order to see total fulfillment. Do you have the fortitude to wait on the Lord? If you feel called to preach, don't quit your job, leave home, and believe God will open some mysterious door! God will open the right door when the time is right. Do what you are supposed to do until the appointed time.

Christ has the key of David and can open and close any door He desires (Rev. 3:8). Ruth was about to walk through the greatest door of her life!

CHAPTER 17

APPOINTMENT WITH DESTINY

NAOMI KNEW THE TIME HAD COME FOR A BREAK-through for herself and for Ruth. Boaz was the kingdom connection who could make it happen. A great restoration of what had been lost was coming. Naomi now had faith. A spark of hope was restored, and Naomi's creativity began to flow. She began to plot a strategy for Ruth and Boaz to come together. Boaz could redeem the lost property for Naomi, and Ruth was the key to open the door to Boaz's heart!

The critical time came at the end of the harvest as the reapers were winnowing. This is a process where the wheat and the chaff are separated. The process is performed at night when the wind picks up. The harvested sheaves are thrown into the wind. As the breeze hits the sheaves, the chaff is blown away as the coveted grain falls to the threshing floor.

The troubles and trials we experience in life eventually bring us to the threshing floor. This is where the good and bad, the wheat and the chaff, are separated. In each of us there exists positive and negative personality traits. We learn them in life through circumstances and encounters with people.

Naomi was bitter due to her problems. That bitterness had to be sifted from her life. Likewise, you and I must be sifted so that the chaff in our lives can be removed. It is at that point that God can truly bless our lives like never before.

A Breakdown Comes Before a Breakthrough

Mark this down. Prior to your major *breakthrough*, there will be a major *breaking down* of your will.

This breaking down is used by God to mold your character. Somewhere in this process, there will be a long night when the wind is contrary to you. When Jesus told His disciples they were going to the "other side" of the sea, the Bible says "a great windstorm arose" (Mark 4:35–37).

The storm hit in the darkest hour of the night. The devil was trying to prevent the disciples from *going over*; instead, he was trying to take them under. Yet God used the wind to display His power. Even the stormy winds obey His voice.

The separation of the wheat from the chaff occurs at night when the wind blows and the darkness has settled around you. You cannot discern what is happening at the time, but those small storms and long nights alone are removing the impurities from you, so the fruit of the Spirit can come forth (Gal. 5:22–23). Boaz (Jesus) must separate the good from the bad, the wheat from the chaff, in order to bring you to the hundredfold blessing!

We must take a trip to the threshing floor in order to become everything God intends. The chaff could be pride, rebellion, or stubbornness. It could represent something that, if it surfaced down the road, could ruin your family, life, or ministry. When John the Baptizer described Christ's ministry, he said:

> His winnowing fan is in His hand, and He will thoroughly clean out His threshing floor, and gather His wheat into the barn; but He will burn up the chaff with unquenchable fire.
> —MATTHEW 3:12

What weakness do you have that raises its head from time to time? Do you have a short fuse in dealing with people? Are you quick to judge things prematurely? Do you, like Tarzan jumping from tree to tree, jump from mood swing to mood swing because of things you like and don't like? Before God uses you on a large scale, before He brings millions of dollars into your business, you will spend some nights on the winnowing floor!

Frustrations are not always caused by blatant sin or hidden sins. Often the little foxes spoil the vines. Undesirable personality traits, feelings, and opinions are like the chaff to the barley. In the grain there is precious fruit the farmer has worked so hard to produce. Yet the outside is a hard shell, the chaff, which must be broken off in order to yield the barley.

Likewise, the chaff in our lives must be broken off so that we can produce the fruit that God desires in our lives. The process of moving from blessing to blessing and climbing from thirtyfold to one hundredfold is connected to your ability to accept godly correction. Perhaps you will have to spend a night on the threshing floor. You may have to wrestle with an angel all night, as Jacob had to, or intercede all night in a garden, as Christ did!

Get Down on the Floor

Naomi understood what Ruth had to do and gave the young woman some life-changing instruction. Ruth's appointment with destiny had arrived. It was her time to get on the threshing floor.

> Therefore wash yourself and anoint yourself, put on your best garment and go down to the threshing floor; but do not make yourself known to the man until he has finished eating and drinking.
>
> —RUTH 3:3

Naomi understood men. To get a man's attention, don't distract him when his attention is focused on something else. There is a time to talk details and get down to business. Let the man finish his work for the day and eat a good meal. Men are more content after their bellies are full.

Herod had a feast and was having such a good time he gave a woman the head of John the Baptist on a silver plate! When a man is content and happy, he will give a woman just about anything she wants.

The Bible says that a woman from Lebanon came to Jesus requesting prayer for her daughter. Because of her Gentile nationality, Christ refused to hear her. She appealed to the disciples and was rejected by them as well. Jesus went so far as to tell her He couldn't give the children's bread to the dogs. Despite these setbacks, the woman began to worship the Lord (Matt. 15:21–28). Worship gets God's attention! The Lord is still seeking those who will worship Him (John 4:23).

The woman replied, "Yes, Lord, yet even the little dogs eat the crumbs which fall from their masters' table!" (Matt. 15:27). She was saying, "I may be a Gentile dog, but I don't need the whole loaf. All

I need is a crumb from the Master's table!" She knew that the substance of the whole loaf could be found in the crumbs as well.

Her words moved Jesus! Remember, faith can be heard in what you say! Some people go to the Lord in prayer and immediately say, "Help! I want. Give me and give us." Jesus began prayer by bragging on His Father. "Our Father in heaven, hallowed be Your name" (Matt. 6:9). Worship is the gateway to the heart of God.

God moves toward us when we minister to Him. As the worship of the Syro-Phoenician woman moved the heart of Jesus, He immediately moved to help the woman's daughter. Likewise, a man will move heaven and earth to help the woman he loves when she brags on him!

The Bible said that "Boaz had eaten and drunk, and his heart was cheerful" (Ruth 3:7). Ruth was instructed to make her move after Boaz had cleared his mind from the day's work and had eaten a good meal. Naomi told Ruth to wash herself. She had to look her best. She wasn't to go to Boaz smelling like a grain silo, but to approach him in a feminine manner.

Ruth was a worker, but she was also a young lady. She was all woman. If Boaz was attracted to Ruth in the field, he would be more impressed when she was dressed up and looking like a lady! Naomi then said, "Get thee down to the floor" (Ruth 3:3, KJV). This is where the breakthrough comes—when we get to the floor on our knees in prayer, and spend time with our heavenly Boaz!

It was time to get down to business, down to where the rubber meets the road. This was the hour of decision. This was the time for divine reversal. It was the moment both Naomi and Ruth needed in order to change their destiny. Boaz was the man to do it.

Yet in order to receive a complete hundredfold blessing, you have to spend time with Boaz on the floor. This is not intended to sound crude or carnal. In the spiritual application, spending time on the floor is spending time in deep intimate prayer and worship before the Lord.

Ruth had known Boaz as a stranger, then as the boss of her workplace, and as a unique friend. Spurred on by Naomi, Ruth was now moving the relationship to another level.

Naomi gave Ruth explicit instructions about what to do when she entered Boaz's presence. Specifically she told her that she was to mark the spot where Boaz lay.

On this particular night Boaz chose to lie down for the night near a pile of grain. In ancient Israel the enemy would often invade the land after the grain was at the threshing floor. The Philistines watched the Hebrews till the ground, plant the seed, water the soil, pull out the weeds, and then harvest the barley and wheat.

Then when the Hebrews took the grain to the threshing floor, the enemy would steal the grain, thus robbing the farmer of his increase and his finances. Remember, the devil never plays by the rules. He comes "to steal, and to kill, and to destroy" (John 10:10). The enemy will let you plant the seed and get to the brink of your harvest, then suddenly bring a problem that will eat your finances and steal the blessing you have been waiting for.

The threshing floor is a place of battle. Boaz was sleeping near the pile of grain in order to protect it from any invader who might come at night! By Ruth coming to the floor, she was showing him again that as he protected the grain, she was willing to be by his side! The battle at the threshing floor turned into the blessing at the threshing floor.

The Time of Testing

Christ revealed to Peter that "Satan has asked for you, that he may sift you as wheat" (Luke 22:31). Jesus said Satan wanted to sift Peter's faith (v. 32). All spiritual testing is designed to sift your faith. God sends a test to build your faith and character, but Satan sends a test to destroy your faith in God.

Satan told God that if He pulled the rug out from under Job and took his financial blessing, Job would lose his faith and curse God. When Job lost his wealth and his children, his wife encouraged him to curse God, but he continued in his faith (Job 2:9–10).

When the test comes at the threshing floor, Satan intends to come and rob you of your blessing, wrecking your confidence in God's provision. On the other hand, God may allow the test to remove the chaff from your spirit and instill character in your life!

Peter's time of testing came *before* he was used to head the Jewish church in Jerusalem. Job's testing came *prior* to his *double portion blessing* in Job 42:10. Ruth had to be steadfast and faithful, *then* the Lord brought her to the floor of Boaz.

> Then it shall be, when he lies down, that you shall notice the place where he lies; and you shall go in, uncover his feet, and lie down; and he will tell you what you should do.
>
> —RUTH 3:4

Uncovering the Feet of Boaz

Naomi predicted that when Ruth uncovered the feet of Boaz, he would tell her what to do. There is something about the feet that is special to God. Feet that carry the good news of the gospel are blessed (Isa. 52:7; Rom. 10:15)! A woman broke open an alabaster box and washed Jesus's feet with her tears (Luke 7:38).

A New Testament word for worship means, to "kiss toward." In one instance where David speaks of worship, the word means to "bow toward." Worship involves a mental and physical prostration before God. When John saw the vision of Christ in Revelation 1:17, he "fell at His feet as dead." In the four Gospels people who needed a miracle would fall at the feet of Jesus.

It was customary in the Middle East for a guest to remove his shoes when he entered a house, and the woman of the house would bring a basin and wash his feet. To exemplify the need for humility in a believer's life, Jesus, the Creator of the universe, washed the feet of His disciples. To wash someone's feet, one must bend down in an act of humility.

The time has come to return to some all-night prayer meetings where we lie on the floor in the presence of God, worshipping at His feet. If we do so, we can arise from the floor knowing we have been changed!

We could call it a Jacob encounter. The old patriarch didn't like what he saw in himself, so he wrestled an angel until sunrise. By the time it was over, he had a new name and a different walk. It's time to get down on the threshing floor with Boaz.

It Came to Pass at Midnight

Midnight is the turning point. Changes occur at midnight! The death angel came into Egypt at midnight (Exod. 12:29). Paul and Silas sang at midnight until the walls of the prison were shaken to the ground (Acts 16:25). As darkness settled over Bethlehem, and the full moon hung over the rugged Judean mountains, Ruth quietly made her way toward the threshing floor. As she stealthily approached Boaz, she knelt and uncovered his feet. It appears he didn't realize she was there for some time. Have you prayed and felt as if God was paying you no attention?

> Now it happened at midnight that the man was startled, and turned himself; and there, a woman was lying at his feet. And he said, "Who are you?" So she answered, "I am Ruth,

your maidservant. Take your maidservant under your wing, for you are a close relative."

—RUTH 3:8–9

As Ruth lay at his feet, Boaz spoke a blessing over her:

Then he said, "Blessed are you of the LORD, my daughter! For you have shown more kindness at the end than at the beginning, in that you did not go after young men, whether poor or rich."

—RUTH 3:10

Boaz described Ruth as a virtuous woman. Because of her obedience and dedication, she received two blessings. First, Boaz announced he would perform the rite of the kinsman-redeemer, then she received another unexpected blessing.

So she lay at his feet until morning, and she arose before one could recognize another. Then he said, "Do not let it be known that the woman came to the threshing floor." Also he said, "Bring the shawl that is on you and hold it." And when she held it, he measured six ephahs of barley, and laid it on her. Then she went into the city.

—RUTH 3:14–15

If we pray and labor in private, we will be rewarded openly. Ruth's story bears this out. Ruth began her labor in a small corner of the field. She then progressed to "handfuls of purpose." Ultimately she went home betrothed to Boaz and her veil overflowing with grain!

Boaz had decided that the time had come to "lay it on her." It was time to honor this woman for her obedience to God! This reminds me of the verse in Luke which says:

Give, and it will be given to you: good measure, pressed down, shaken together, and running over will be put into your bosom. For with the same measure that you use, it will be measured back to you.

—LUKE 6:38

- Good measure is the thirtyfold level.

- Pressed down and shaken together is the sixtyfold level.

- Running over is the hundredfold level.

Ruth went from "just enough" to "enough and then some" and finally to the level of "more than enough." God brought increase! Because of Ruth's encounter with Boaz, He then performed the rite of the kinsman-redeemer!

The Kinsman-Redeemer

If a husband died and there were no men in the family to inherit his land, the woman was to marry the brother of her husband in order to carry on the family name. If there were no brothers, then a next of kin could marry the woman and redeem the family inheritance. Since Boaz was a near kinsman, he had the right to redeem the land that belonged to Elimelech and Naomi.

Boaz called a meeting at the city gate and informed the people that if no one else was going to redeem the property of Elimelech, he would. As it turned out, there was a kinsman who was a closer relative than Boaz, but he was not willing to marry Ruth. This relative deferred to Boaz, who was more than willing to marry her. To legally close the deal, at the gate of the city, Boaz exchanged shoes with the other kinsman.

When God Gets in Your Shoes

Now this was the custom in former times in Israel concerning redeeming and exchanging, to confirm anything: one man took off his sandal and gave it to the other, and this was a confirmation in Israel.

—RUTH 4:7

The exchanging of shoes meant, "Now I have a right to walk where I haven't walked before. I have legal authority to step into territory that I couldn't before!" Years before this, God had told Moses to remove the shoes from off his feet (Exod. 3:5). The ground was holy, God said. Therefore, out of respect, Moses removed his shoes. Years ago I saw another reason why Moses removed his shoes. The job God had for Moses was too big for one man. God was saying, "Moses, get your shoes off and let Me get in them! Let Me walk in your shoes down to Egypt!" More than forty years later God told Joshua to remove the "shoe" (singular) from off his foot. Notice that God said *shoe,* not *shoes* (Josh. 5:15).

Joshua knew the ground was holy, and that the "Commander of the army of the LORD" was in the camp to bring a victory strategy in taking down the walls of Jericho (Josh. 5:14). If we understand the law of exchanging a shoe, God was saying, "Joshua, I am about to give you this land. I am redeeming back this land for My people. Give Me your shoe, and I will release legal authority for you and all of Israel to walk through the land and to claim it back for your people!"

We need for God to step in our shoes. At times things we attempt to accomplish are bigger than we are. They are bigger than our ability, bigger than our budget, and bigger than our faith! When we let God take over the situation, then we can declare, "The walls are bigger than I am able to scale, and the enemy is stronger than I am able to beat, but God can go with us and defeat the enemy!"

From a Pauper to a Princess

As Boaz pulled off his shoe (sandal), Ruth and Naomi experienced their biggest breakthrough in ten years! The inheritance of her husband that was lost was now restored. Something of great value had been redeemed! When you control the walk, you don't always move in the right direction, but when God gets in your shoes, He will always bring you to blessing and favor.

Once Boaz married Ruth, she was immediately exalted to a position of prominence. Instantly the entire city knew who this woman was. The women of the city spoke that they wanted Ruth to become like Rachel and Leah—the two matriarchs who birthed the nation of Israel (Ruth 4:11–12). Ruth did not gain the attention and affection of Boaz by chasing him around like a young girl who has a crush on a boy; neither did she flirt with him or gain favor by bragging on his physical appearance, or his physical frame. In fact, in that culture all of these would have been considered forward and rebuked by the man and women in the city. Ruth simply worked her job, focusing upon her mother-in-law, and God brought her husband to her. In her exaltation she never forgot Naomi. In fact, she stayed connected to Naomi in a personal, intimate way. When Ruth's son, Obed, was born, it was Naomi who took the child and became his nurse, or nanny. It was a son. Naomi didn't get another son for Ruth to marry, but she was in charge of a son of destiny.

As Obed grew, perhaps Naomi told the child the story of the journey from Moab to Bethlehem, of God's provision and his mother's love story. Naomi had quite a heritage to pass on to her grandson and, for that matter, to the world. If Naomi had written a book, perhaps it would have been called, *From Moab to Bethlehem—From Tragedy to Triumph!*

Never forget who helped you to get where you are today. For me, it was pastors from small, rural churches who gave a teenage kid preacher an opportunity to minister in their small congregations. At times older, gray-haired men will stop in our ministry headquarters. They will ask to see me, informing the receptionist, "When Perry was just a kid he preached in my church." I always stop what I am doing, go to the lobby and hug these older saints, and allow them to reminisce about a black-haired, skinny preacher who held for them the best revival the church ever had. At times I just go back and cry to see what God has done.

Who was your helper? Was it a mother or father who worked two jobs to help you through school? Was it your wife or husband who believed in you when nobody else did? Did a pastor continue to encourage you when others said you would never make it? Was the person a special kingdom connection God sent to connect you with other people? Never forget the Jerichos and Moabs from where you came and the men and Naomis who were there for you when you had little or nothing. Don't dwell on the past, but if you remember where you were you can better appreciate where you are going.

A Prophetic Utterance Came to Pass

The inhabitants of Bethlehem spoke a prophetic word over Ruth and Boaz. They declared that their names would be "famous" in Bethlehem and in Ephratah (Ruth 4:11). This prophetic word was spoken at a time when there was no Book of Ruth in the holy Scriptures. However, multiple millions have read this love story, teaching and preaching it for generations. When reading the first few verses in Ruth, we see death, separation, and sorrow. When we read the last few verses in the same book, we see victory, success, and life.

The marriage of Boaz and Ruth produced a son named Obed, and Obed had a son named Jesse. It was Jesse whose son was David (Ruth 4:20–22). This is the same David who many years later was anointed to be king over all of Israel, and the same David to whom the promise of the Messiah was given.

In retrospect, look back on the number of lives impacted by one scarlet thread! The town prostitute of Jericho converted to the Hebrew God, marrying one of the two spies. As Israel took the land, the tribe of Judah took the area of Bethlehem-Judah. Rahab and her husband settled in this region, obtaining a huge inheritance of farm land. It was their son, Boaz, who married Ruth the Moabite, bringing her into the covenant of Abraham and the Mosaic Law of God. From the lineage of Rahab and Ruth came David, the man to whom the seed of the Messiah was promised. Christ was required by the prophets to be born in the tribe of Judah, in Bethlehem (Mic. 5:2). Those living in Bethlehem were farmers and shepherds, from Boaz to Jesse to David. The Messiah would use the analogy of a farmer to teach His followers and would identify Himself as the Great Shepherd. Bethlehem raised lambs for the temple sacrifices, and the grains were used for the table of showbread. David's seed, Christ the Messiah, was the Lamb of God who would take away the sins of the world (John 1:29), and was the true bread that came from heaven to feed men (John 6:32).

Your scarlet thread is your *faith* that holds on to a promise when the town is shaking and walls are falling all around you. Your scarlet threat is your *prayers* that your entire family will come into the kingdom and be preserved from the outside battles that are destroying others. Your scarlet thread is tied around your *trust* that God's plan for the future is greater than Satan's plans of the past. Your scarlet thread is what you hold on to when you are tying it around someone you love, holding the rope, sticking to your prayers and confessions, until you can lift them from the pits of despair and destruction. From one act of faith—a scarlet thread in a window—a family legacy was forged. You can do the same with your scarlet thread.

NOTES

Chapter 1
A Praying Mother Was a Common Thread

1. *Against All Odds: In Search of a Miracle* created and produced by Bill McKay (N.p.: American Trademark Pictures, 2006), DVD.

Chapter 2
The Jewel From Jericho

1. Jericho Municipality, "History," http://www.jericho-city.org/etemplate.php?id=15 (accessed June 8, 2014).

2. Bryant Wood, "The Walls of Jericho," Answers in Genesis, March 1, 1999, http://www.answersingenesis.org/articles/cm/v21/n2/the-walls-of-jericho (accessed June 8, 2014).

3. Alpha Omega Institute, "The Crimson or Scarlet Worm," http://www.discovercreation.org/newsletters/TheCrimsonOrScarletWorm.htm (accessed June 8, 2014).

4. Israelcraft, "Tallit Blue Threads," http://www.israelcraft.com/tallit-information/tallit-blue-threads.html (accessed June 8, 2014).

5. The Temple Institute, "In Search of the Tola' at Shani—The Crimson Worm," http://www.templeinstitute.org/tola-at_shani.htm (accessed June 8, 2014).

6. Jacob Neusner, *Narrative and Document in the Rabbinic Canon* (Lanham, MD: University Press of America, 2010), 129.

Chapter 3
Jael and Judith—Nailing Trouble in the Head

1. Bruce Wilkinson, *The Prayer of Jabez* (Sisters, OR: Multnomah Publishers, 2000).

2. Yishai Chasidah, *Encyclopedia of Biblical Personalities* (Brooklyn, NY: Shaar Press, 1994).

3. Ibid., 129.

4. The New American Bible, "The Book of Judith" (New York: Oxford University Press Inc., 2001), 460, http://tinyurl.com/bookofjudith (accessed June 8, 2014).

5. Ron Wolfson, Joel Lurie Grishaver, ed., *Hanukkah: The Family Guide to Spiritual Celebration* (Woodstock, VT: Jewish Lights Publishing, 2001).

Chapter 5
The Power of a Mother's Prophecy

1. David Edwin Harrell Jr., *Oral Roberts: An American Life* (Bloomington, IN: Indiana University Press, 1985).

2. This story was related personally to the author by Mark Casto.

3. This story was related to the author by Dr. E. L. Terry in the 1980s, as Dr. Terry was the minister when this amazing incident occurred.

4. This story is the testimony of Terry Lamunyon, who is a full-time worker at VOE and OCI Ministry in Cleveland, Tennessee.

Chapter 6
From the Womb of Mercy

1. George Washington, *Quotations of George Washington* (Carlisle, MA: Applewood Books, 2004), 7.

2. *Do Not Disturb* (blog), "Understanding 'Love': Racham," May 16, 2012, http://donotdisturbblog.com/2012/05/16/understanding-love-racham/ (accessed June 9, 2014).

3. Trent C. Butler, ed., s.v. "Compassion," *Holman Bible Dictionary*, http://www.studylight.org/dictionaries/hbd/view.cgi?n=1369 (accessed June 9, 2014).

4. NewAdvent.org, "The History of Joseph the Carpenter," http://newadvent.org/fathers/0805.htm (accessed June 9, 2014).

5. JewishEncyclopedia.com, "Nicodemus," http://www.jewishencyclopedia.com/articles/11525-nicodemus (accessed June 9, 2014).

6. HaDavar Messianic Ministries, "You Must be Born Again," http://www.hadavar.org/getting-to-know-god/you-must-be-born-again/ (accessed June 9, 2014).

Chapter 7
Preparing to Battle Seven End-Time Spirits

1. W. E. Vine, *Vine's Expository Dictionary of the Old and New Testament Words* (Nashville, TN: Thomas Nelson, 2003), s.v. "reject," 519.

Chapter 8
Waiting Long for an Answer

1. W. E. Vine, *Vine's Expository Dictionary of New Testament Words* (Minneapolis, MN: Bethany House, 1984).

2. Albert Barnes, "Commentary on Daniel 4:1," *Barnes' Notes on the New Testament*, http://www.studylight.org/commentaries/bnb/view .cgi?bk=26&ch=4 (accessed June 9, 2014).

3. Ibid.

Chapter 10
Five Crazy Prayers to Pray When Your Family Is in Trouble

1. Albert Barnes, "Commentary on Ephesians 5:14," *Barnes' Notes on the New Testament*, http://www.studylight.org/commentary/ephesians/5-14.html (accessed June 9, 2014).

2. Wikipedia.org, "Just Say No," http://en.wikipedia.org/wiki/Just_Say_ No (accessed June 9, 2014).

3. Dean Edell, "Why Didn't the 'Just Say No' to Drugs Campaign Work?," HealthCentral.com, July 20, 1999, http://www.healthcentral.com/ drdean/408/14392.html (accessed June 8, 2014).

4. Wikipedia.org, "This Is Your Brain on Drugs," http://en.wikipedia .org/wiki/This_is_your_brain_on_drugs (accessed June 9, 2014).

5. YouTube.com, "CDC: Tips from Former Smokers—Terrie's Ad," https://www.youtube.com/watch?v=5zWB4dLYChM (accessed June 9, 2014).

6. *Winston-Salem Journal*, "Anti-Smoking Activist Terrie Hall Dies," September 16, 2013, http://www.journalnow.com/news/local/article_ aa2cfe4c-1f2a-11e3-8cf0-0019bb30f31a.html (accessed June 9, 2014).

7. Wendy Koch, "Diseased Ex-Smokers Testify in Graphic Anti-Smoking Ads," *USA Today*, March 28, 2013, http://www.usatoday.com/story/ news/nation/2013/03/28/cdc-anti-smoking-ads/2018121/ (accessed June 9, 2014).

Chapter 12
Paul and Esther—Preparation for Destiny

1. This information about Vernon and Elvis Presley was related directly to the author by M. H. Kennedy in the late 1970s when he was the state bishop for the Church of God denomination in Virginia.

2. This was the testimony of Donnie Sumner, whom the author met in Tennessee in the mid-1980s.

3. The source has requested that the author not comment more on this as there is a plan to release certain information unknown to the general public in the future.

Chapter 13
Breaking Satan's Strongholds on Your Bloodline

1. *Autism Society*, "Facts and Statistics," http://www.autism-society.org/about-autism/facts-and-statistics/ (accessed June 9, 2014).

2. ANSWER Aspergers Network Support, "Statistics," http://www.aspergersmn.org/what-is-aspergers/statistics (accessed June 9, 2014).

Chapter 14
Rizpah—Dealing With the Birds and the Beasts

1. Abarim Publications, "Meaning and Etymology of the Name Rizpah," http://www.abarim-publications.com/Meaning/Rizpah.html#.U5ZrhXJdVow (accessed June 9, 2014).

2. Biblehub.com, s.v. "morag," http://biblehub.com/hebrew/4173.htm (accessed June 9, 2014).

3. "Rock of Ages, Cleft for Me" by Augustus Montague Toplady, public domain.

Chapter 16
The Bethlehem Love Triangle

1. Susan Adams, "New Survey: Majority of Employees Dissatisfied," May 18, 2012, *Forbes*, http://www.forbes.com/sites/susanadams/2012/05/18/new-survey-majority-of-employees-dissatisfied/ (accessed June 10, 2014).

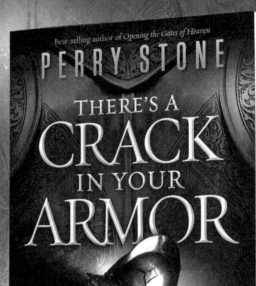